Emotional Intelligence for Military Leaders

The Pathway to Effective Leadership

Gerald F. Sewell, Lieutenant Colonel, USAR (ret)

Copyright © 2014 Gerald F. Sewell

All rights reserved.

ISBN-10: 1500742856
ISBN-13: 978-1500742850

DEDICATION

To all those on the front lines, to those who have served and to those who have made the ultimate sacrifice.

CONTENTS

Page

Purpose: *This book provides an overview of why Emotional Intelligence(EI) is important to U.S. Army and other military leaders by offering some basic information on where and how EI can make a difference in military organizations. This is not meant to be the end all of Emotional intelligence for the Army, it is merely a start in raising the awareness of military leaders to this valuable and available pathway to effective leadership. The intent is to show how EI can make a positive impact in several key areas of leadership.*

Chapter 1 - Emotional Intelligence for Military leaders   1

This Chapter provides an overview of the importance of Emotional Intelligence to military leaders.

Chapter 2 – Emotional Intelligence and the Army Leadership Requirements Model   8

This chapter provides a brief history of emotional intelligence, takes a look at the Army's Leader Requirements Model as an EI model and makes the case for the need to include EI intentionally as a key aspect of Army leadership. It will also include examples of several EI models and discuss how they can be used by military leaders.

Chapter 3 – From Toxic to Tonic – Emotional Intelligence for the Toxic Leader   41

This chapter highlights the value of emotional intelligence to addressing the problem within the military of Toxic Leadership. It looks at the deficit of emotional skills in some leaders and discusses how to use EI to identify and develop more tonic leaders.

Chapter 4 – Emotional Intelligence, Interdependence and Relationship Building — 53

This chapter examines the value of Emotional Intelligence to relationship building and its importance to military leaders. Chapter four also provides an additional model that helps in understanding the role of Emotional intelligence in building relationships.

Chapter 5 - Emotional Intelligence, Power and Influence — 91

This chapter looks at the application and importance of EI to power and influence. It will address the two types of power, Personal and Position, as identified by French and Raven and also the role of the Army's influence techniques as found in the U.S. Army's Leadership Manual ADRP 6-22.

Chapter 6 – Emotional Intelligence and Resilience in the U.S. Army. — 109

This chapter looks at Emotional Intelligence and Resilience. It discusses how leaders can build resilience and the ability to cope with negative stress in themselves and others using competencies of emotional intelligence.

Chapter 7 – Emotional Intelligence for Military Leaders - Conclusions — 122

This chapter provides summaries of the major points from each preceding chapter.

Notes - 126

Emotional Intelligence for Military Leaders

ACKNOWLEDGMENTS

Thanks to: Dr. Jack Kem, of the U.S. Army's Command and General Staff College, who first told me to write. To Dr. Ted Thomas of the same institution, who encouraged me to pursue and write about the things that I think are important, and to my dear wife, Roann, who knew I really wanted to do this and kept encouraging me to finish.

To my God and King who loves me and gives me Life.

1. EMOTIONAL INTELLIGENCE FOR MILITARY LEADERS

"The Army will produce professional leaders that practice the mission command philosophy whether conducting unified land operations or Army generating force functions. These leaders <u>possess emotional intelligence</u> and achieve credibility with external JIIM partners, allies, internal agencies, and stakeholders."

Army Leader Development Strategy 2013 p.6

So what is Emotional Intelligence (EI) and what is it good for? Professors, Peter Salovey of Yale University and John D. Mayer of the University of New Hampshire in a 1990 paper on the subject defined it as "The subset of social intelligence that involves the ability to monitor one's own and other's feelings and emotions, to discriminate among them and to use this information to guide one's thinking and actions."[1] Daniel Goleman, the psychologist, journalist, and author whose 1995 best seller was the vehicle that catapulted EI into the mainstream writes, "Emotional intelligence is the capacity for recognizing our own feelings and those of others, for motivating ourselves, and for managing emotions well in ourselves and our relationships."[2] These are but two of a variety of definitions and EI constructs. But they all, no matter the semantics, are saying the same thing. It's all about the emotions; understanding them and applying that understanding to improve ourselves and our relationships. Therefore, it is not at all debatable that Goleman and Salovey and Mayer and the rest of the experts are speaking of the very skills that make leaders successful; these EI skills are the critical interpersonal skills that are key competencies for military leaders.

The Army Leader Development Strategy 2013, quoted in the header, is correct in identifying the need for Army leaders to be emotionally intelligent. Our opening quote seems to indicate an embracing of emotional intelligence (EI) by the Army's leadership. Unfortunately that is the only place in the strategy's 24 pages that EI is mentioned. Not a ringing endorsement, but it is a great step in the right direction. So what is the Army's position on emotional intelligence? What does the Army do with it? What can the Army do with it? How can Army leadership be enhanced by Emotional intelligence? This book provides answers to these questions and information on how the Army and other military organizations can and should embrace emotional intelligence. It also addresses the benefits of doing so. It looks at key areas in which emotional intelligence can be of valuable help to the Army and other military services. Chapter two makes the case that the Army should intentionally include EI as a key leader competency. It also makes the argument that the Army already has an EI model.

Emotional intelligence impacts a wide range of leadership functions. Leaders that have a high degree of emotional intelligence understand that EI enhances every area of leadership and organizational function. It increases the likelihood of effective and successful relationships, teams and organizations. Daniel Goleman writes in a 2004 edition of the Harvard Business review, "I have found, however, that the most effective leaders are alike in one crucial way: They all have a high degree of what has come to be known as emotional intelligence. It's not that IQ and technical skills are irrelevant. They do matter, but mainly as "threshold capabilities"; that is, they are the entry-level requirements for executive positions. But my research, along with other recent studies, clearly shows that emotional intelligence is the sine qua non of leadership. Without it, a person can have the best training in the world, an incisive, analytical mind, and an endless supply of smart ideas, but he still won't make a great leader."[3] This also holds true for military leaders. We place great value in the military threshold capabilities; the technical and tactical proficiency of our military leaders, and reward them accordingly with promotions and positions of increased responsibility and prestige, but we pay little attention to what really makes them successful - their ability to understand and apply the intangible skills of leadership that are represented by emotional intelligence. There is no record of a longitudinal study having been conducted within the military to determine the impact of emotional intelligence on leader success, however anecdotal evidence reveals that the military's truly successful leaders possess a high degree of emotional intelligence.

So, what is emotional intelligence and why does the Army need it? Dr. Goleman writes, in his 1998 book, *Working with Emotional Intelligence*, "Emotional intelligence is the capacity for recognizing our own feelings and those of others, for motivating ourselves, and for managing emotions well in ourselves and our relationships."[4] He further clarifies that for leaders in his 2002 book, *Primal Leadership*, "Emotional intelligence is how leaders handle themselves and their relationships."[5] Emotional intelligence enables the understanding of the social skills necessary to discern and apply the appropriate influence techniques in the variety of situations and contexts leaders must face. Emotional intelligence also facilitates the ability to establish mutually beneficial relationships. This ability, long referred to in the Army as tact and interpersonal skills, is in fact the skills and competencies of emotional intelligence.

The Army's Leader Development Strategy 2013 (ALDS 2013) has correctly identified the need for EI in Army leaders. Emotional intelligence should be an integral part of the Army's leader development program. Embracing the attributes and skills of emotional intelligence are critical to all aspects of a leader's development, particularly in the leadership domains of self awareness, social understanding and applying influence.

Understanding emotional intelligence is necessary in all areas that involve leading and managing people and organizations. It can be a valuable asset at every level of leadership. It is a helpful tool in a number of areas which this book will cover. These include: EI as a key leadership competency, EI and Power and influence, EI and relationship building, and the value of EI in building and maintaining resiliency.

Before we launch into a discussion of how military leaders can use Emotional Intelligence we must first establish if they are even interested. Chapter two makes the case that the U.S. Army already has a model of emotional intelligence.

2. EMOTIONAL INTELLIGENCE AND THE ARMY LEADERSHIP REQUIREMENTS MODEL

> *"Emotional intelligence is the "capacity for recognizing our own feelings and those of others, for motivating ourselves, and for managing emotions well in ourselves and our relationships."*

Daniel Goleman in *Emotional Intelligence: Why It Can Matter More Than IQ*, 1995

> *"Broadly speaking, emotional intelligence addresses the emotional, personal, social and survival dimensions of intelligence, which are often more important for daily functioning than the more traditional cognitive aspects of intelligence...."*

Reuven BarOn, PhD. in the *BarOn EQ-I Technical Manual, 2004*

Introduction: It's not an Oxymoron.

Is there a role for Emotional Intelligence (EI) in United States Army leadership? Is military leadership incompatible with the concept of emotional intelligence? Is EI too soft? Are Army leaders too hard? Is leadership in the Army too mechanical; developed by receiving instruction in leadership styles and management processes and studying the leadership techniques of great military leaders? Is there a need within military leadership for Emotional Intelligence? The answer to our last question, which fuels the response of the rest, is a resounding yes! If Army leaders are really interested in effective leadership they will embrace this key ingredient to successful relationships which underscores all organizational success. The most valuable element in building and maintaining successful relationships, individual or team, is Emotional Intelligence.

This chapter presents how the U. S. Army has integrated emotional intelligence into its leadership doctrine but, does not intentionally advocate its application, thereby not encouraging its leaders to use this valuable leadership enhancer as they develop Army organizations and teams; as well as their personal leadership. To effectively draw on the influence of emotional intelligence Army leaders must understand what it is and how the current Army leadership doctrine aligns with the elements of EI and current EI thought as well as take steps to apply it holistically in leader training and education.

Army Leadership Defined

Army Leadership is more than X's and O's, more than emotionless structured leader development programs, more than leadership study and analysis and more than the stereotypical coercive motivation. Army leadership is, according to the Army's leadership doctrinal manual, Army Doctrinal Reference Publication 6-22 (ADRP 6-22), "The process of influencing people by providing purpose, direction, and motivation while operating to accomplish the mission and improve the organization".[6] What is missing from the definition and the manual is a holistic emphasis on the emotional side of leadership. Emotional not in the sense of the hyper-excited leader banging on the desk, or screaming at new recruits, or the much tabooed "touchy feely" leader; but leaders aware of their own emotions and how they impact their behavior and relationships with those around them as they undertake the daily missions and tasks assigned them. According to Psychologist and author Daniel Goleman, in order for a leader in any type of organization to be successful, he must exercise and be aware of his emotions and how his emotional competence influences the way he leads and impacts his followers.[7]

ADRP 6-22 outlines the attributes and competencies required of Army Leaders. But who makes up the Army's corps of leaders? The ADRP tells us an Army leader is anyone who by virtue of assumed role or assigned responsibility inspires and influences people to accomplish organizational goals. Army leaders motivate people both inside and outside the chain of command to pursue actions, focus thinking, and shape decisions for the greater good of the organization.[8] The general public's idea of an Army leader is the crusty old NCO or the charismatic officer leading troops into battle or the well decorated general giving the highly inspirational speech. However, based on the Army's definition, it's leaders are any person that satisfies the responsibilities within that definition; that is soldiers, civilians, non-commissioned officers, warrant officers and commissioned officers; the full gambit of personnel in the Army system. The Army recognizes that every person has the ability and potential to be a leader. All of the Army's leaders can benefit from a greater understanding of their emotions and the emotions of others.

Emotional Intelligence: A Brief History

Emotional Intelligence, although not found in any implicit form in the Army's doctrinal manuals, is hardly a new field of study; it is based on a long history of research and theory in the fields of Psychology, Human Intelligence and the Social Sciences. In his 1983 book, *Frames of Mind*, Howard Gardner, a psychologist at the Harvard School of education, indicates that the study of the emotional side of intelligence can be traced back to the early 1800s through the early studies of Franz Joseph Gall and his associate Joseph Spurzheim as they identified the presence in the brain of several affective faculties such as; reverence, self-esteem and reflective powers.[9] Dr. Reuven BarOn, author and developer of the Emotional Quotient Inventory (EQ-i), in his *EQ-i Technical Manual* identifies David Wechsler and his studies on "the nonintellective aspects of general intelligence conducted in 1940"[10] as the foundation in the advancement of the study of emotional intelligence. Some of the most notable groundbreaking work in the field was done by Gardner. In *Frames of Mind*, Gardner proposed that there was not just one type of intelligence (IQ), which led to success in life, but there was a wide spectrum of intelligences and within those intelligences there were at least 4 varieties of interpersonal intelligence. [11] In *Frames of Mind*, Gardner identifies and discusses his 6 different types of intelligence; Linguistic Intelligence, Musical Intelligence, Logical-Mathematical Intelligence, Spatial Intelligence, Bodily-Kinesthetic Intelligence, and Personal Intelligence.

Within his Personal Intelligence realm Gardner writes of two types of personal intelligence that both deal with the emotions; he speaks of them as the internal aspects of a person, intrapersonal intelligence, and the other personal intelligence which turns outward, to other individuals, interpersonal intelligence[12] Gardner's' groundbreaking work was further developed by Yale Psychologist, Peter Salovey. Salovey's conceptualization of EI included; appraising the emotions in self and others, regulating emotions in self and others and using emotions in adaptive ways.[13] These were identified and described in his 1990 study, conducted with an associate, Peter Mayer. The term Emotional Intelligence was also introduced in this study.[14]

Psychologist, Daniel Goleman, popularized Emotional Intelligence with his landmark book of that name as it became a household expression as well as a field of study worth consideration in the business, academic and social science communities. Goleman developed his thought and theory about emotional intelligence through his research in more than 200 organizations. Goleman explains that without it, a person can have first class training, an incisive mind, and an endless supply of good ideas, but he still won't make a great leader.[15] Supported by his research, Goleman maintained that despite the cognitive intelligence and business smarts of executives and managers, they could not have gained their levels of success if they did not possess good skills in the area of emotional intelligence[16]. In his initial research and theories, Goleman adopted a five domain model based on the findings of Salovey and Mayer. He has since modified those domains to four[17].

Although recognized as the catalyst and one of the leading voices in the Emotional Intelligence community, Goleman's construct is not the only EI model, nor is it the definitive thought on emotional intelligence. This chapter also discusses another popular model; the BarOn Emotional Intelligence model developed by Dr. Reuven BarOn for his emotional intelligence assessment tool, the BarOn Emotional Quotient Inventory (EQ-i). Later chapters also present several other constructs and theories. Dr. BarOn's model presents 5 Realms of Emotional Intelligence with 15 scales. Both constructs align with the Army's Leadership Requirements Model.

The Models

The Goleman Model

Highlighted in Figure 1 are Goleman's 4 EI domains and their associated competencies. These domains; Self-Awareness, Self-Management, Social-Awareness, and Relationship Management and their associated competencies, according to Goleman, provide leaders with a sharper understanding of how leadership works and assists them in leading more effectively.[18] Figure 1 provides a listing of each of the EI domains and their associated competencies as identified by Goleman and company in his 2002 book, *Primal Leadership*. Written with co-authors, Richard Boyatzis and Annie McKee, Goleman incorporates the domain of empathy as identified in his benchmark 1995 book, *Emotional Intelligence*, into the domain of Social Awareness thus leaving four overarching domains.

Emotional Intelligence
Domains and Competencies
Goleman Model

Personal Competence		Social Competence	
Self Awareness	**Self - Management**	**Social Awareness**	**Relationship Management**
– Emotional Self-Awareness – Self Assessment – Self Confidence	– Emotional Self-Control – Transparency – Adaptability – Achievement – Initiative – Optimism	– Organizational Awareness – Service – Empathy	– Inspirational Leadership – Influence – Developing Others – Catalyst for Change – Conflict Management – Teamwork-collaboration

Figure 1. Goleman Model of Emotional Intelligence Domains and Competencies

Goleman's four EI domains and 18 leadership competencies, although described here in these summary definitions from Wikipedia[19] align with the broader definitions from BarOn's EQ-I Technical Manual. The first domain is **Self Awareness,** described in short definition as the ability to read one's emotion and recognize the impact while using "gut feelings" to guide decisions. Self Awareness includes the competencies of emotional self-awareness, accurate self-assessment, and self-confidence. The second domain is **Self-Management**. It involves the controlling of one's emotions and impulses and adapting to changing circumstances. Self management includes the competencies of emotional self-control, transparency, adaptability, achievement, initiative, and optimism. The third domain is **Social Awareness.** Social Awareness is the ability to sense, understand, and react to others emotions while comprehending social networks. Social Awareness includes the competencies of empathy, organizational awareness, and service. The fourth and final domain is **Relationship Management**. This is the ability to inspire, influence and develop others while managing conflict. Relationship management includes the competencies of inspirational leadership, influence, developing others, being a catalyst for change, conflict management, and teamwork/collaboration.

In *Primal Leadership* the authors place the domains into two areas of emotional achievement that they ascribe to individuals as they acquire mastery of each domain - Personal Competence and Social Competence. Mastery of domains one and two, which the authors place under the umbrella of personal competence, depends heavily upon listening to one's self, becoming aware of one's emotional state, values, standards, and impact upon others. Self-examination and gathering feedback about oneself through coaching and 360 reviews assist with the development of personal competence. Mastery of domains three and four, which the authors describe as social competence, flows from empathic listening and resonating to others' thinking to develop one's thoughts and actions, which enables a leader to provide both unified and individual senses of direction for his or her group. Empathic listening is a skill that requires a basic level of understanding along with regular practice.[20]

The BarOn Model

The BarOn Model composed of five composite realms and their 15 associated scales differs from the Goleman model in that all but one of its realms deals with social competency as defined by Goleman. The Interpersonal realm identified by BarOn inherently captures the social competencies of Goleman while BarOn's Intrapersonal, Adaptability, Stress Management and the General Mood realms all focus on the personal competencies. However, the last three provide focus on personal areas not explicitly identified in the Goleman construct. The four domains of the Goleman model focus on the two major areas of Personal and Social management; with its 18 competencies all pointing to one or the other of these two major areas, while in the BarOn model the interpersonal realm provides the importance and understanding of relationships and responses to others with the other four realms emphasizing the importance of knowing and managing one's own emotions as the key to orderly and effective relationships. The 5 Realms of the BarOn construct and their descriptions as found in Stein and Books' *The EQ Edge*[21] are; the **Intrapersonal Realm**, which involves what we generally refer to as the "inner self." It determines how in touch with your feelings you are, how good you feel about yourself and about what you're doing in life. Success in this area means that you are able to express your feelings, live and work independently, feel strong, and have confidence in expressing your ideas and beliefs. The scales under this realm include; Self-awareness, Assertiveness, Independence, Self-Regard and Self Actualization. The **Interpersonal Realm** involves what are known as people skills – your ability to interact and get along with others. It includes the scales of Empathy, Social responsibility and Interpersonal Relationships. The next realm, the **Adaptability Realm,** involves your ability to be flexible and realistic, and to solve a range of problems as they arise. Its three scales are Reality Testing, Flexibility and Problem Solving. The **Stress Management Realm** concerns your ability to tolerate stress and control impulses. Its two scales are Stress Tolerance and Impulse Control. The final realm is the **General Mood Realm**. Its two scales describe this realm, the scales of Optimism and Happiness.

BarOn Model of Emotional Intelligence

INTRAPERSONAL	INTERPERSONAL	ADAPTABILITY	STRESS MANAGEMENT	GENERAL MOOD
– Emotional Self-Awareness – Assertiveness – Independence – Self-Regard – Self-Actualization	– Empathy – Social Responsibility – Interpersonal Relationship	– Problem Solving – Reality-Testing – Flexibility	– Stress Tolerance – Impulse Control	– Happiness – Optimism

Figure 2, The BarOn Model of Emotional Intelligence.

While both EI models provide implications for all leaders, the realms of the BarOn Model provides added emphasis and relevance to military leaders; providing valuable awareness and tools for utilizing and enhancing each scale. The Adaptability and Stress management scales specifically address competencies necessary for growth in decision making, flexibility in thinking and action and managing stress, all key attributes for military leaders. As you will see later in the comparison, even though the LRM includes competencies and attributes that correlate to both models, they each provide some unique scales and competencies which can provide valuable areas of study for Army leaders as they seek to be more effective.

Emotional Intelligence in U.S. Army Leadership Doctrine

The United States Army has long recognized that its success depends upon its people. The age old army maxim, "Mission First, People always", is not just lip service. The Army spends an exceptional amount of time emphasizing the importance of leader to follower relationships, teamwork and espirit de corps as well as the importance of organizational climate. Each of these issues intrinsically requires the components of emotional intelligence and will be enhanced by a holistic inclusion of those EI components in leader training as well as in the doctrine and leadership literature.

As discussed earlier, the primary source of the Army's

preferred leadership skills and characteristics, including the emotional intangibles, are found in ADRP 6-22, the U.S. Army's leadership publication. The ADRP does not limit its discussion of the emotional aspects of leadership to the Leadership Requirements Model. Paragraph headings that sound like emotional intelligence competencies can be found throughout the manual; there are paragraphs that address soldier and leader self-awareness, the *emotional factors* [my emphasis] of leadership (these include self control, stability and balance)[22] as well as interpersonal tact, adaptability and judgment. In these sections the manual defines and provides brief explanations of the importance of the particular factors to leaders.

    The Army, despite not presenting EI as an integral part of leader effectiveness, does in its current leadership doctrine promote self aware, adaptive, flexible and agile leaders. Each of these elements are competencies of emotional intelligence. This provides further recognition of the importance of emotional intelligence to the effectiveness of Army leaders. The Army's leadership doctrine describes its leaders as self-aware and innovative in ADRP 6-22). The ADRP identifies the importance of self-awareness, 'Self-awareness has the potential to help all leaders become better adjusted and more effective. Self-awareness is relevant for contemporary operations requiring cultural sensitivity and for a leader's adaptability to inevitable environmental change."[23] Daniel Goleman identifies Self Awareness as the foundation for the rest of the EI competencies.[24]

What 6-22 doesn't do is threefold: 1. Acknowledge the attributes and competencies of the LRM as the emotional elements they are, thereby removing the implication that they are hard skills, 2. Discuss the importance of understanding and applying the emotional aspects of leadership, and 3. Discuss how to develop the emotional skills necessary to successfully employ the many facets of the emotions. Taking these steps will enhance the leadership publications and doctrine and will provide valuable assistance to Army leaders in becoming emotionally intelligent and more effective.

In June of 2008, the Army published its study on the Human Dimension in Full Spectrum Operations (2015-2024). The title of this particular pamphlet is promising to those interested in the people aspects. However, despite its title, it is not a manual which discusses the emotional aspects of soldiers and leaders in peace or in combat where the emotional skills advanced by emotional intelligence are particularly critical to understanding how soldiers react as well as how to help them develop resiliency. The pamphlet identifies the human dimension as comprising the moral, cognitive, and physical components of Soldier and organizational development and performance essential to raise, prepare, and employ the Army in full spectrum operations.[25] However within the pamphlet several aspects of emotional intelligence are addressed. In the study the Army identifies the need for leader self awareness and acknowledgment of this characteristic in others. The study also identifies the need for the socialization process of soldier to leader and leader to soldier identification, both elements of emotional intelligence.[26] Also mentioned, in the pamphlet's discussion of the human spirit, is the individual need to develop a broad concept of social awareness.[27] Identifying these elements as important to the 'human dimension is an important first step. The next step must be to provide a holistic application of these elements and others under the umbrella which they fall into, emotional intelligence. The study authored by the Army's Training and Doctrine Command (TRADOC), the military authority responsible for all Army training and leader development, continues the broad brush effect of FM (ADRP) 6-22 in addressing the emotional aspects of soldiers and leaders. The ten chapter TRADOC pamphlet only briefly touches upon self awareness and empathy (a competency and scale of the Goleman and BarOn models respectively) in its chapter 9, which discusses the requirements and responsibilities of leadership. Unfortunately the Army's human dimension does not and is not intended to address the whole person; rather it is based on a holistic view of how humans function in a system. These systems include environment, culture, community, politics and society, among others. [28] The TRADOC pamphlet defers to the Army's FM 6-22 for the impact of leadership on the human dimension; stating, "For Leadership weaves throughout this concept both explicitly and implicitly. FM 6-22 describes leadership in detail and from many perspectives. Rather than restate this information, this chapter assumes that the essence of leadership is immutable, and that the characteristics the Army wishes to develop in leaders at all levels will not change significantly."[29] Those "characteristics" identified in FM 6-22, as attributes and competencies, are the elements that hold the key to the application of emotional intelligence in the Army's leadership doctrine.

Emotional Intelligence and the Army Leadership Requirements Model

In ADRP 6-22, the Army defines, outlines and describes its leadership doctrine. The foundation of this philosophy is highlighted in the Army Leadership Requirements Model (LRM). In the LRM the Army identifies the attributes and competencies required for successful leaders. The LRMs' attributes and competencies parallel the EI constructs of Goleman and BarOn. A side by side comparison and analysis of the attributes and competencies of the Army's doctrine and the EI models show the Army's inclusion of the discipline of EI into the Army leadership doctrine through the leader attributes and competencies chosen. This analysis begins with an explanation of the attributes and competencies and then provides a crosswalk of their correlation to the Domains and Realms of our two models of emotional intelligence discussed earlier in this chapter.

The Army's Doctrinal Reference Publication, (ADRP) 6-22, *Army Leadership-Competent: Confident, and Agile,* outlines the Army's current doctrine on leadership. Published initially in 2006 as Field Manual (FM) 6-22, the doctrine underwent a slight revision and renaming in 2012 to become ADRP 6-22. It provides a new twist on the Army's historical foundation of leadership; the characteristics that describe what an Army leader needs to Be, Know and Do. Although the Army still defines their leaders implicitly in light of Be, Know Do; Be- the characteristics and attributes a leader must have; Know - the skills and knowledge they must possess and develop, and Do - how they in turn operate with those attributes and skills and knowledge; they no longer stress the leadership doctrine in those terms. In the 2006 rewrite, the Army determined that it was more important to doctrinally place the emphasis on leader intangibles, in the sense of leader attributes and in the leader skills in terms of the competencies that a leader must have. In its new doctrine, or the redefining of the old leadership doctrine, the Army leadership experts have developed a leadership requirements model designed around the Leadership Attributes, the new "Be" and Leadership Competencies, the new combined "Know and Do." The following chart, the Leadership Requirements Model, found in ADRP 6-22, identifies the Leadership Attributes and Competencies for Army leaders at all levels.

The Army Leadership Requirements Model

ATTRIBUTES

CHARACTER	PRESENCE	INTELLECT
*Army Values *Empathy *Warrior Ethos/Service Ethos *Discipline	*Military and professional bearing *Fitness *Confidence *Resilience	*Mental Agility *Sound judgment *Innovation *Interpersonal tact *Expertise

LEADS	DEVELOPS	ACHIEVES
*Leads others *Builds trust *Extends influence beyond the chain of command *Leads by example *Communicates	*Creates a positive environment/ Fosters esprit de corps *Prepares self *Develops others *Stewards the profession	*Gets results

COMPETENCIES

Figure 3. Leadership Requirements Model from ADRP 6-22

ADRP 6-22 provides the following description of the model and additional definition of its component attributes and competencies and their relationship to each other. "The model's basic components center on what a leader is and what a leader does. The leader's character, presence, and intellect enable the leader to master the core leader competencies through dedicated lifelong learning. The balanced application of the critical leadership requirements empowers the Army leader to build high-performing and cohesive organizations able to effectively project and support land power. It also creates positive organizational climates, allowing for individual and team learning, and empathy for all team members, Soldiers, civilians, and their families.[30] A more detailed description of each of the attributes and competencies are provided in the associated sections and chapters within the publication.

The core leader competencies emphasize the roles, functions, and activities of what leaders do. The action-based competencies do not include attributes of character.[31] The core leader competencies are complemented by attributes that distinguish high performing leaders of character. Attributes are characteristics that are an inherent part of an individual's total core, physical, and intellectual aspects. Attributes shape how an individual behaves in their environment.[32]

Inherent in each of the Attributes; What an Army Leader is, and the Competencies, What an Army Leader Does, are the elements of Emotional Intelligence as defined and described by Goleman and BarOn. If Army leaders are to be truly successful at the art of leadership they must understand the linkage and how to maximize their emotional intelligence. The attributes and competencies are compatible with the Goleman model and fit neatly into the domains of Emotional Intelligence. The following crosswalk discusses the placement of the LRM attributes and competencies within the appropriate domains of the Goleman model.

The LRM and Goleman Model Crosswalk

When aligned with the Goleman model, the 12 elements of the Army leadership Attributes, appropriately align within Goleman's domains with crossover into both personal and social competence areas with the attributes and competencies. Seven of the 12 attributes fit nicely into the personal competence area as they deal specifically with the personal characteristics of the individual leader and what a leader must be (see figure 4). The ten Leadership competencies fit into both sides of the chart but more importantly each of the 10 leadership competencies fall under the Relationship management domain as they plainly relate to establishing relationships and dealing with others (see figure 4). The comparison demonstrates the emotional aspects of the leader attributes and competencies as they clearly correlate with the EI competencies of the Goleman model.

LRM and Goleman Model Crosswalk

Attributes and <u>Competencies</u>

Personal Competence		Social Competence	
Self-Awareness	**Self-Management**	**Social Awareness**	**Relationship Management**
– Emotional Self-Awareness – <u>Self-Awareness</u> – <u>Self-Assessment</u> – <u>Prepares Self</u> – Self-Confidence – *Composed, Confident* – *Warrior Ethos* – *Domain Knowledge* – *Military Bearing*	– Emotional Self-Control – Transparency – Adaptability – *Resilient* – *Mental Agility* – Achievement – Initiative – *Innovation* – Optimism – <u>Creates a positive environment</u> – *Physically Fit*	– Organizational Awareness – *Army values* – Service – Empathy – *Empathy*	– Inspirational Leadership – <u>Leads by example</u> – Influence – <u>Extends influence</u> – <u>Leads Others</u> – <u>Communicates</u> – Developing Others – <u>Develops Leaders</u> – <u>Stewards the Profession</u> – <u>Builds Trust</u> – Catalyst for Change – <u>Creates a positive environment</u> – Conflict Management – *Interpersonal tact* – *Sound Judgment* – Teamwork-collaboration – <u>Gets Results</u>

Figure 4. LRM and Goleman Model Crosswalk

The LRM and BarOn Model Crosswalk

The LRM crosswalk with the BarOn model provides a placement of the LRM attributes and competencies in the appropriate realms they would appear in as BarOn scales or as they would support the development of elements within each realm. The attributes and competencies are identified as indicated in the chart title. The crosswalk is found in figure 5 below. The BarOn model recognizes the importance of the individual effectively managing her own emotions in order to interact effectively with others and understand the emotions of others. With the exception of the Interpersonal realm each of BarOn's realms is focused on the individual managing aspects of his own emotions. The 12 elements of the Army Leader Attributes appropriately align throughout the model with crossover into both interpersonal and self management areas with only one of the competencies (Prepares Self) identified in this realm (see figure 5). This is appropriate as the attributes identify what characteristics the individual leader must have. The other eleven fit neatly into the remaining realms of the BarOn model supporting the assigned realms. Three attributes from the LRM address the Intrapersonal Scale with one competency also highlighted in the self management area. The remaining seven competencies are spread throughout the chart. The leader competencies fit into both sides of the chart but more importantly each of the 10 leader competencies fall within the relationship management domain as they clearly enable leaders to lead by establishing effective relationships.

LRM and BarOn Crosswalk

Attributes and <u>Competencies</u>

INTRAPERSONAL	INTERPERSONAL	ADAPTABILITY	STRESS MANAGEMENT	GENERAL MOOD
– Self-Awareness – <u>Prepares Self</u> – Assertiveness – Independence – Self-Regard – Self Actualization – *Leads by Example* – *Mental Agility* – *Self-Awareness* – *Military Bearing*	– Empathy – Social Responsibility – Interpersonal Relationship – Empathy – <u>Develops Leaders</u> – *Interpersonal Tact* – <u>Leads Others</u> – <u>Communicates</u> – <u>Extends Influence</u> – <u>Gets Results</u>	– Problem Solving – Reality-Testing – Flexibility – *Sound Judgment* – *Innovation* – *Mental Agility* – *Domain Knowledge*	– Stress Tolerance – Impulse Control – *Resilient* – *Composed* – *Physically fit* – *Warrior Ethos*	– Happiness – Optimism – *Composed, Confident* – <u>Creates a Positive Environment</u>

Figure 5. LRM/BarOn Crosswalk

This crosswalk of the BarOn and Goleman models establishes correlation of the Army Leader Attributes and Competencies with the elements of Emotional intelligence in these two popular models. Emotional intelligence is about understanding your own emotions and those of others in order to be a more successful person. The Leader attributes and competencies assist leaders in becoming better leaders by understanding themselves and their relationships to others as they lead people and organizations. The Army's Leader development programs will do a great service to its leaders by placing increased emphasis on the emotional intelligent aspects of leadership.

It's not an Oxymoron.

The Army in its current leadership framework does not holistically address the importance of the emotional side of leadership. Despite this the LRM's leadership attributes and competencies demonstrate the U.S. Army's application of the importance of emotional intelligence to Army leaders. The correlation and relationships of the elements of Emotional Intelligence and the Army Leadership Requirements Model are clear: inherent in the attributes and competencies are emotional aspects that when understood and employed lead to effective leadership. The next step for the Army is to holistically incorporate Emotional intelligence in its leader and soldier development programs. Army leaders studying and applying emotional intelligence will be more effective and successful in building strong teams and organizations.

3. FROM TOXIC TO TONIC – EMOTIONAL INTELLIGENCE FOR THE TOXIC LEADER

"The Army will produce professional leaders that practice the mission command philosophy whether conducting unified land operations or Army generating force functions. These leaders possess emotional intelligence and achieve credibility with external JIIM partners, allies, internal agencies, and stakeholders."

The Army Leader Development Strategy 2013 p.6

As the U.S. Army continues to adjust its leader Development strategy in the years ahead, if the ALDS 2013 quote in Chapter one is any indication, emotional intelligence will quickly become an integral part of developing Army Leaders. This chapter provides answers to one critical area where Army leader development can benefit from emotional intelligence. This area is illustrated in the following vignette.

The Toxic Leader

The battalion Live Fire Exercise (LFX) had not gone as well as desired. The leadership was anxious as they prepared to brief the new brigade commander on the details of the validation training exercise. The core of the battalion's NCO and officer leadership was comprised of solid and experienced combat veterans who were finally coming together after a tumultuous and frenetic reset phase. In his guidance prior to the exercise, the legendary Colonel M.D. "Mad Dog" Brooks, the new Brigade Combat Team (BCT) Commander, had been very direct and precise about the live-fire exercise tasks, conditions and standards he expected. He left little latitude for initiative and no margin for error. His intent was to get the unit back to the "highest level of proficiency as quickly as possible," and everyone in the battalion understood that he was not satisfied with their current performance.

Administrative and maintenance problems plagued the exercise from the beginning, and many of them contributed to the failure to achieve the exacting training timeline established by the BCT staff. Unreliable range targets, crew-served and individual weapons malfunctions, vehicle operational readiness, and delays in the ammunition draw all combined to keep the unit off-schedule from the start. Through the sheer force of the battalion's leaders, every company completed all of the training tasks. The Observer

Controllers rated their gunnery skills and fire discipline as exceptional. Although the battalion's Soldiers and junior leaders had some significant gaps in their tactical skills, they had just proven that they could still shoot, move and communicate like real warriors.

As anticipated, the After Action Review (AAR) began badly. After the fourth slide, COL Brooks' visible agitation transitioned to anger and he erupted. He retrieved a stack of 3x5 cards from his breast pocket, and summarily listed all the things the battalion had done wrong. He berated the battalion and company commanders as failures in front of everyone present. In concluding, he said, "Your leadership incompetence is exceeded only by your collective inability to meet training timelines, maintain your equipment and weapons to standards, and conduct basic range administrative procedures!" When the senior OC attempted to interject with the positive aspects of their highly successful gunnery results, Brooks immediately cut him off by stating, "Major, when I want you're your opinion I will ask for it. Until then, keep your mouth shut!"

Not allowing the briefing to continue, COL Brooks ordered the battalion to remain in the field until its problems were fixed. He abruptly left the briefing area, not bothering to talk further with the battalion commander or even the BCT S-3.[33]

Colonel Brooks, the brigade commander in our vignette, exhibits the characteristics of the classic military toxic leader. The good news is that the military, particularly, the U. S. Army has taken some serious steps to address "toxicity" in its leaders. The Army defines toxic leadership to a large degree as it has been defined by retired Army Colonel George Reed in his 2004 article in *Military Review*. Reed believes toxic leaders all possess a combination of three key elements.[34]   These are:

1. An apparent lack of concern for the well-being of subordinates.

2. A personality or interpersonal technique that negatively affects organizational climate.

3. A conviction by subordinates that the leader is motivated

primarily by self-interest.

The U.S. Army leadership has embraced this definition and instituted reforms in its leader evaluation systems which are designed to identify these individuals and hopefully get them to change or get them to leave. ALDS 2013 identifies the intent of these changes:

"We are also implementing 360° assessments which include input not only from superiors but also peers and subordinates. Such a system will help individual leaders identify strengths to sustain and weaknesses to eliminate."[35]

The Toxic Impact

The problem with toxic leaders is not that they have toxic personalities, but it is the impact on others that their attitude and behavior and produces; and this is usually manifest by way of negative emotions. Dan Goleman writes in *Primal Leadership*, "Negative emotions – especially chronic anger, anxiety, or a sense of futility – powerfully disrupt work, hijacking attention from the task at hand."[36] These negative emotions often cause distraction, and the negative moods that deter individuals from applying their best effort as fear of incurring the wrath of the toxic leader. The negative moods that accompany a toxic environment prohibit individuals from doing their best work. Constant negative pressures and attitudes cause excessive distress which further deteriorates the performance in the work place. Studies show that US industry loses millions of working days and billions of dollars each year from employee absenteeism due to stress.[37] How does this translate in the military environment in which military personnel are not likely to experience this high absenteeism? It becomes more a case of mental and emotional absenteeism as opposed to being physically missing from the work place. Toxic leadership acts as a strong toxin and has the potential to, as pointed out in *Primal Leadership*, poison the emotional climate of the organization[38]. The climate that toxic leadership creates is one that is totally detrimental to effective functioning, builds negative stress and causes individuals to "check out."

The U.S. Army leadership definition calls for leaders to accomplish the mission and improve the organization.[39] A critical part of improving the organization is developing soldiers and leaders. Toxic leaders, though often adept at accomplishing the mission, due to their deficits in emotional intelligence, fail epically at the personnel development tasks.

How Emotional Intelligence can help

Toxic leadership as defined by Colonel Reed is a product of a lack of individual Self Awareness and Self Management as well as the lack of or inattention to Social Awareness and Relationship management skills. These four characteristics and skills represent the four domains of emotional intelligence as defined by Dr. Goleman. Goleman's domains, as summarized from *Primal Leadership*[40], are described below with the application to Colonel Reeds 3 Characteristics of the toxic leader.

Goleman's domains are: Self-Awareness, described in short

definition as the ability to read one's emotion and recognize the impact while using "gut sense" to guide decisions. Self-Awareness includes the competencies of emotional self-awareness, accurate self-assessment, and self-confidence. Toxic Leaders lack the ability to conduct the self assessment required by Self Awareness. This deficiency feeds an unbalanced ego and also, according to Colonel Reed's characteristics, fosters *"the apparent lack of concern for the well being of subordinates."* Self-Management is the second domain. It involves the controlling of one's emotions and impulses and adapting to changing circumstances. Self-management includes the competencies of emotional self-control, transparency, adaptability, achievement, initiative, and optimism. Toxic leaders often exhibit a deficit in emotional self-control as they employ, according to Colonel Reed, *"a personality or interpersonal technique that negatively affects organizational climate."* Social Awareness the third domain is the ability to sense, understand, and react to others emotions while comprehending social networks. Social Awareness includes the competencies of empathy, organizational awareness, and service. Toxic leaders are lacking in all of the competencies and behaviors of this domain. This is displayed by the Toxic leader as in their self absorption he or she is not concerned with the emotions or well being of others. The fourth and final domain is Relationship Management. This is the ability to inspire, influence and develop others while managing conflict. Relationship management includes the competencies of inspirational leadership, influence, developing others, being a catalyst for change, conflict management, and teamwork/collaboration. Relationship management skills are necessary to reverse each of the toxic leader characteristics.

The first step in any personal development program is self-awareness. Leader's have to identify their developmental gaps, accept them and then design the necessary steps to growth. The Army's 360 assessment program is a great tool to help toxic leaders recognize the dangers of their toxicity and in some cases the fact that they are toxic or is perceived so by their subordinates, peers and/or superiors. Once leaders embrace this understanding they can then begin to address the needs. The next step must be an honest assessment of a leader's emotional intelligence skills. There are a number of emotional intelligence assessments and self evaluation tools available to help leaders identify and measure the emotional intelligence skills they may need to develop. The ultimate goal for all leaders must be to develop or enhance their emotional intelligence skills. To this end most of the assessment tools currently available also provide a process to assist the individual in developing their EI skills, with or without a coach/trainer.

The Army has recognized the importance of Emotional intelligence in its leaders and at several levels has instituted training and awareness in emotional intelligence. The Army's Command and General Staff College (CGSC) runs a two hour seminar on emotional intelligence at its School for Command Preparation (SCP) for command designees at the Battalion level. CGSC's Command and General Staff Officer's Course, for Majors, c includes reference to EI throughout its leadership curriculum and includes a 24 hour elective course, entitled Emotional Intelligence for Leaders. In this course field grade leaders discuss the application of EI to various aspects of leadership and have the opportunity to perform an individual EI skills assessment followed by guided interpretation of results with development and execution of developmental action plans to enhance their emotional intelligence skills.

Emotional intelligence is not magic, but....

Emotional intelligence is no magic formula, but the understanding and practice of EI by Army leaders will go a long way in promoting self awareness and social awareness in leaders at all levels and all Army cohorts. This will subsequently decrease the levels of toxicity in Army formations and lead to more effective leaders and more efficient organizations. The Army leadership has it right; Army leaders must possess emotional intelligence in order to effectively lead Regionally Aligned Forces in the joint and multinational coalitions of the future.

Gerald F. Sewell

4. EMOTIONAL INTELLIGENCE, INTERDEPENDENCE, AND RELATIONSHIP BUILDING

Emotional intelligence is the capacity for recognizing our own feelings and those of others, for motivating ourselves, and for managing emotions well in ourselves and our relationships.

—Daniel Goleman in Emotional Intelligence: Why It Can Matter More Than IQ, 1995

Emotional intelligence is concerned with understanding oneself and others, relating to people, and adapting to and coping with the immediate surroundings to be more successful in dealing with environmental demands.

—Reuven BarOn, Ph.D. in the BarOn EQ-I Technical Manual, 2004

We define emotional intelligence as the subset of social intelligence that involves the ability to monitor one's own and others' feelings and emotions, to discriminate among them and to use this information to guide one's thinking and actions."

-Peter Salovey and John Mayer, Emotional Intelligence, 1990

Introduction – Emotional Intelligence and Relationships

In their illuminating text, *"What We Know about Emotional Intelligence"*, Zeidner, Matthews and Roberts, within their discussion of the state of the art in scientific research on emotional intelligence, address three conflicting ways of understanding emotional intelligence.[41] The authors discuss three distinctive models. Their implication is that all EI theories and scientific as well as

non-scientific conceptions fit into one of these three models. The authors label the first of these models The Ability model. This model favors defining emotional intelligence as an ability resembling other standard intelligences.[42] They cite the construct introduced by Peter Salovey and John Mayer, in their 1990 paper on emotional intelligence, as a typical example of Ability models. They call a second type of model The Mixed Model, because it includes both abilities and qualities such as personality and motivational traits.[43] They present Daniel Goleman's Model, introduced first in his groundbreaking book, *Emotional Intelligence* in 1995 and since refined in His 2002 *Primal Leadership*, collaboration with Richard Boyatzis and Annie McKee, as the typical Mixed Model. They also suggest that Reuven BarOn's construct presented in his *Emotional Quotient-inventory Technical Manual* is a mixed model. Their final model type is that of Trait Emotional Intelligence. Zeidner, et.al, do not present an example here but writes of the theory: 'Trait emotional intelligence represents an overarching personality factor that represents the person's emotional self-confidence.[44] It obviously supports the theory that individuals are born with certain traits and/or personality factors that add to or detract from their emotional intelligence. These "state of the art" models though possessing conflicting ways of understanding emotional intelligence, all have a common theme surrounding the value and purpose of emotional intelligence. This common theme is evidenced by the three quotes at the front of this article. The mixed models represented by the Goleman and BarOn quotes, clearly identify this theme while the abilities model, represented by the Salovey and Mayer quote, strongly implies the same. That theme is twofold; first, it recognizes that individuals must possess self-awareness; this involves knowledge of, acknowledgment of, and sought after understanding of one's own strengths, weaknesses, and emotions, and second, each person needs to also be alert to the same trio of intra/interpersonal attributes in others, those they interact with, in order to display empathy towards them as they seek to understand them. These statements recognize that everything we do impacts not only ourselves but others as well. They further recognize that we can do nothing without the necessary partnerships spawned by a fundamental human interdependence. Arguably everything we do requires interaction with others, direct or indirect. Whether we are operating on behalf of ourselves or collaborating with a team to accomplish a common goal, we need other people. Therefore we must be constantly mindful of and attentive to the relationships we have with the people around us.

To this end the key phrase from the Goleman definition that supports this chapter's purpose is; "*… for managing emotions well in ourselves and our relationships.*" The BarOn definition though slightly different affirms the focus on relationships. The same theme can be interpreted from the Salovey and Mayer definition as well. They write that emotional intelligence is the ability to monitor one's own and others' feelings and emotions, to discriminate among them and to use this information to guide one's thinking and actions.[45] Salovey and Mayer's theory is based on the ability to recognize, read and regulate the emotions; ones' own as well as others. Although it differs in its application and measure, this theory's key aspect agrees with both Goleman and BarOn in that it recognizes the importance of the application of the role of emotions and emotional intelligence in understanding others - inherently . . . to develop relationships.

This chapter explores the concept of human interdependence as it applies to the need for relationship and introduces and discusses the Human Interdependence model of emotional intelligence. It stresses the importance of emotional intelligence as the key element in building and sustaining relationships. This chapter also discusses a variety of emotional intelligence models as tool chests available to facilitate building healthy, supportive and sustainable relationships.

Human Interdependence in Maslow's Hierarchy of Needs

"Interdependence is and ought to be as much the ideal of man as self-sufficiency. Man is a social being. Without interrelation with society he cannot realize his oneness with the universe or suppress his egotism. His social interdependence enables him to test his faith and to prove himself on the touchstone of reality.

Mahatma Gandhi, Young India, March 21, 1929, p. 93[46]

    In the above quote, the venerated, Mahatma Gandhi recognizes that man is a social creature and thus without his apprehending a set of basic social needs, through the recognition and acceptance by other social creatures, he cannot reach his "oneness." Gandhi further identifies a major problem with the lack of relationship when he references the need to suppress man's egotism. Without serious relationship with others; recognizing the importance of and value of each person, egotism could potentially run out of control. Gandhi's "oneness", described as Self-Actualization in Abraham Maslow's theory of Human Motivation, is considered the ultimate goal of human-motivation, and as such is situated at the top of Maslow's hierarchy of needs. Maslow writes of self-actualization; a musician must make music, an artist must paint, a poet must write, if he is to be ultimately happy. What a man can be, he must be. This need we may call self-actualization.[47] As we strive for "self-actualization" or as an old U.S. Army jingo used to coin, "to Be all you can be," we seek relationships that provide us recognition, companionship, esteem and help that will motivate us to that end. The ultimate goal of self-actualization is positioned at the pinnacle of the hierarchy, just above the basic needs of belonging and esteem. The basic needs of belonging and esteem, highlights man's interdependent nature; in his drive to reach the ultimate personal need, humankind must achieve these two fundamental needs that are impossible without interaction with other people. These last two needs which cannot be attained without interdependence make up the last two steps to the top of the pyramid.

However, first things first; let us take a look at interdependence and two different yet similar definitions. The first, a scientific definition, identifies that interdependence is when living things rely on others for their existence. If one of the organisms were to die, so would the other because they cannot live independently.[48] To survive, to find meaning in their existence, strength and sustenance; these "organisms" must have relationship with other like organisms. That is not to say that humans are like "micro-organisms" that cannot literally survive without the biological and chemical interdependency and benefits they provide to each other, but the point of emphasis here is that humans do need each other to achieve certain basic needs. These needs dictate the interdependence of relationships. Our second definition, taken from the popular Wikipedia encyclopedia, is a purely social relationships definition: "Interdependence is a relationship in which each member is mutually dependent on the others. This concept differs from a dependent relationship, where some members are dependent and some are not. In an interdependent relationship, participants may be emotionally, economically, ecologically and/or morally reliant on and responsible to each other."[49] In the interdependence of our relationships we must rely on each other to fulfill our esteem and belongingness needs.

Abraham Maslow identifies this basic need for human interaction in the third step of his Hierarchy of Needs model as the need to belong to and be affiliated with a group. His article speaks of belongingness as he addresses the basic need for love in his section on the love needs he writes, *"The love needs. --* If both the physiological and the safety needs are fairly well gratified, then there will emerge the love and affection and belongingness needs, and the whole cycle [p. 381] already described will repeat itself with this new center. Now the person will feel keenly, as never before, the absence of friends, or a sweetheart, or a wife, or children. He will hunger for affectionate relations with people in general, namely, for a place in his group, and he will strive with great intensity to achieve this goal. He will want to attain such a place more than anything else in the world, and may even forget that once, when he was hungry, he sneered at love.[50] Maslow further identified esteem and self-esteem as universal needs. He hypothesized, originally in a 1943 article in *Psychological Review that* everyone prefers to feel important, needed, useful, successful, proud, [and] respected.[51] All of these desires fit into the love/belonging and/or the esteem needs. None of them can be achieved without establishing relationships; thus the interdependence of people - one to another. Maslow recognized this basic need for people to interact with other people (Figure 6 highlights the interdependence of the Belonging and Esteem needs).

Maslow's Hierarchy of Needs

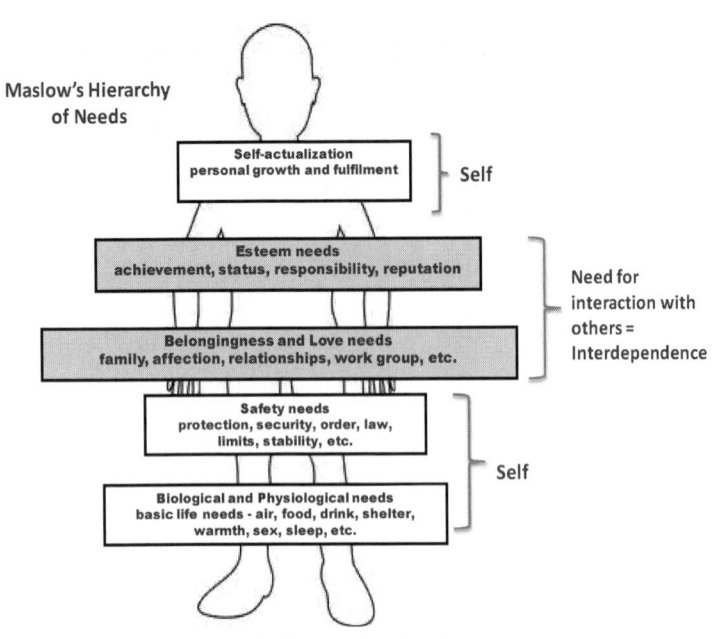

- Self-actualization: personal growth and fulfilment — Self
- Esteem needs: achievement, status, responsibility, reputation
- Belongingness and Love needs: family, affection, relationships, work group, etc.
  — Need for interaction with others = Interdependence
- Safety needs: protection, security, order, law, limits, stability, etc.
- Biological and Physiological needs: basic life needs - air, food, drink, shelter, warmth, sex, sleep, etc.
  — Self

Fig 6.. Maslow's Hierarchy of Needs and Interdependence

Maslow's hierarchy confirms our basic need for human interaction. This interdependency is necessary to allow us to satisfy our belonging and esteem needs. The need for interaction with other humans drives the requirement for the belonging and esteem needs; which can only be fulfilled in the interaction of relationship. Since we need relationships, how do we ensure that the relationships we build are such that they allow us to meet our belonging and esteem needs? How do we ensure they are not just connections of convenience? To the last question - true relationship is beneficial to all parties, there are instances in which convenience is the goal, but these incidents are not genuine because it is not really relationship that is being sought after, it is rather some selfish motive which merely uses others as a means to that end. True relationship is mutually beneficial to all parties. That is the role of emotional intelligence – building mutually beneficial relationships. EI provides tools and platforms for understanding and facilitating the developmental aspects of self and relationships. Self, because I have to first gain a deeper knowledge and understanding of who I am and my needs before I can understand my role in relating to others. Now once I understand my needs and how I must interact with others to acquire those needs, I can then begin to understand how my accomplishing those needs are dependent upon my relationships with others. The first step in developing mutually beneficial, healthy, lasting relationships is to understand the anatomy of relationships.

The Anatomy of Relationships

Every relationship is composed of three basic elements: self, others and the environment. Regardless of the relationship interface these three elements are present. The model at figure 7 provides a depiction of the interface of each element. We will discuss each part in turn.

Human Interdependence Model of Emotional Intelligence

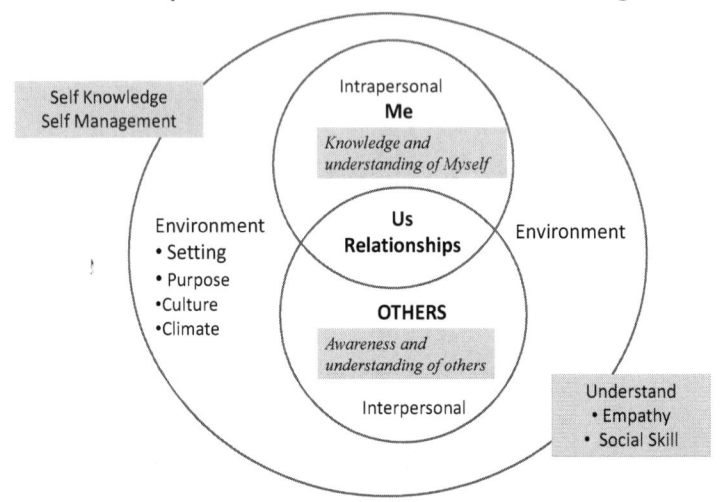

Fig. 7. Human Interdependence Model of Emotional Intelligence

The "me" of Relationship

Every relationship starts with people. People are obviously the most important element in relationships, however just as important are the purpose behind the relationship and the environment in which the relationship building takes place. We will discuss these presently. The people in relationships, as identified in figure 7, are the "me" of relationships, the "other" in the relationship and ultimately us, which speaks to the satisfying or the belonging, love and esteem needs developed through the bonding of relationship. In considering the first person of relationship building, me, the most critical step is the necessity of achieving a practical level of self-awareness. We must first understand the first person of relationships - Me. This starts with asking ourselves, "Do I really know what makes me tick? Do I really understand why I like the things I like, respond the way I respond in various situations? What are my motivations, my preferences, dislikes, idiosyncrasies? I need to do the deep reflection in regards to each of these which allows me to understand who I am, assess if that is really the person I want to be, then identify the gaps between who I am, who I think I am, and who I want to be, and develop strategies, when necessary, to close those gaps. How often do I need to reflect on my self-awareness? This should be an ongoing effort. I should be constantly asking myself, the questions above. This must take place with each interaction. That may seem like a bit too much. I am not advocating that in the midst of a conversation you must stop and list each perspective. But if you have attained a degree of and have a continuing desire for understanding yourself you are more inclined to be attuned to yourself and be aware of how you will, respond as opposed to how you should respond in different environments and situations. This self knowledge will cause you to evaluate the appropriate response and more likely choose the correct response; the response that builds positive outcomes and relationships.

Emotional Intelligence and Self Knowledge.

What are the considerations of and purposes behind self-awareness? Self-awareness is one of the emotional intelligence abilities, competencies or skills (dependent upon which construct you are using) that you will find in each of the three more popular EI models as well as most other models that are currently being used. Daniel Goleman in *Primal Leadership* writes that self – awareness is the foundation for all of the other emotional intelligence domains.[52] Goleman's declaration supports my earlier explanation that understanding and developing self is the foundation of healthy relationships. My self-awareness helps me understand and regulate my behaviors and responses to my environment as well as others. The more I reflect and review my motivations the more I get to know myself. This self-knowledge moves me beyond a cursory awareness of self to a knowledge of myself which allows me to address necessary changes or development. Darwin Nelson and Gary Low in their personal change model (figure 8) identify the cause of all behavior as rooted in our beliefs, values and thoughts attached to an emotional event.[53] If I am not self-aware, if I have not obtained a clear understanding of the origins of my beliefs values and thoughts then I cannot begin to understand the roots of my behaviors and how that will impact my relationships. I cannot begin to regulate my behaviors to insure I am working toward building healthy and mutually beneficial relationships. Once I have a "working" knowledge of myself I begin to apply that self-knowledge to understanding my interacting with others to build solid mutually supporting relationships.

The Change Process

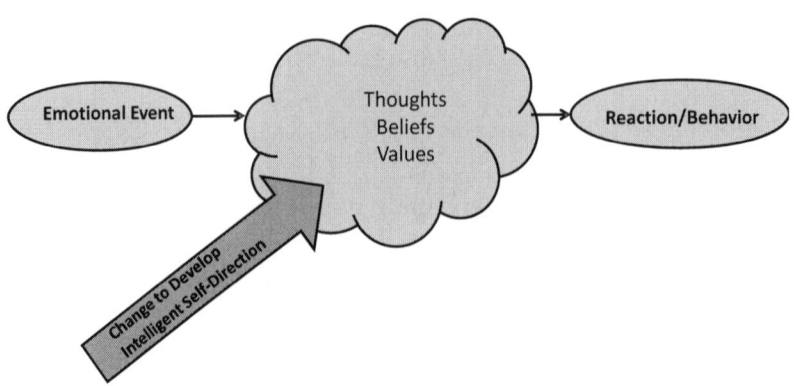

Fig. 8. The Change Process. Darwin Nelson and Gary Low, *Achieving Academic and Career Excellence*, 2011

The 'Others' of Relationship

"First seek to Understand"

In his book, The Seven Habits of Highly Effective People, Steven Covey identifies as Habit #5, First seek to understand and then to be understood.[54] The first part of habit #5, "First seek to understand…" provides the key action needed when we are addressing the second person or persons of relationship, referred to in our model as 'others'.

This step is addressed in most emotional intelligence models as the competency of empathy. There are a number of questions I must ask when I am seeking to understand that other person. These include: What do I know about this other person I am about to interact with? What is their personality like, what are their likes and dislikes? Fortunately, unlike when I examine myself, I really do not need this information as I am entering into a new relationship with others. Often we have some knowledge of other people; however there are certain expectations we have of others that derive from our basic human commonalities. We have a tendency to relate to those like us; and the beginning of every relationship is that the other person is... well a person; so they must like the things I like and respond the way I respond. If this were really the case, however, there would be no need for seeking to understand others, because as I understand myself then I would understand others. The good news is everyone is not like me. Harking back to the Nelson and Low model in figure 8, everyone has different experiences, thoughts, beliefs and values, so we do not automatically respond like everyone else. This is good news; because if we were all the same it would be a very dull world. There are obviously some beliefs and values that may be common, but our behaviors are driven by the elements in Nelson and Low's "cloud." To begin to understand others I need to first acknowledge and accept that their elements in the "cloud" are not necessarily like mine. People are different and different is good. In addition to the cloud elements these differences may include, experience, education, cultural background, nationality, gender and more. Each person must enter the interaction empathically understanding the value of the potential differences before we can begin building a mutually supportive relationship. These relationships do not take place in a vacuum. Essential to the development and growth of relationships is the environment in which they takes place.

The Environment of Relationship

The outer ring in our Emotional Intelligence model (figure 7) depicts the environment as the all encompassing circle in which relationships and relationship building takes place. All of the people elements interact within the constraints of the environment. The environment defines the context in which relationship building takes place. The external issues that impact the interaction of individuals or for that matter groups further define the environment. These issues include, setting, purpose and culture and climate. Let us look at the setting; where is this interaction taking place; is it in an office environment, a restaurant, a classroom, a business trip or is it in an elevator? The location of an interaction can either facilitate or inhibit the development of a relationship. Individuals attending a class are encouraged to develop relationships as they share the same experience. Two individuals on an elevator may exchange a cordial greeting but our mental model of elevator riding often precludes us from making eye contact. We tend to become focused on the slowly changing floor indicators that tell us we are about to find relief as our floor draws near. In a workplace the environment is often defined by a hierarchy of responsibility; thus often dictating how the individuals relate to each other and how relationships are built and developed. The nature of relationships is often dependent upon the needs of the organization and the roles each member plays. The Leaders often identify requirements, set expectations and leave it to the led to get it done. The qualified employee will meet the requirement and move on to the next thing; or the leadership can be very involved in the lives of the workers, having established good supportive relationships which generate successful accomplishment of requirements.

Another element of the environment is the social and/or organizational culture or climate in which the relationship or interaction must take place. Considerations include: what are the expectations of the organization, what are the relationship expectations between leaders and workers? Who can talk to whom? What are the communications expectations in this organization? Are all people considered equal? How do we communicate across departments? Is there a protocol for communicating to external organizations? Are there cultural expectations within each department? These considerations have to also be applied to the climate question, although in many organizations culture and climate are considered synonymous. What about societal culture? Societal cultures also dictate how we interact; what relationships are taboo and what the expectations of building relationships are and how those interactions take place. Within these societies there are also social subgroups that may have their own sub-cultural expectations.

Another critical element of the environment in which relationship building takes place is the purpose behind an interaction. Why are we coming together? What do we hope to accomplish? Can I accomplish this without you? Is it important to me that you are satisfied with the outcome of our interaction? Is it important to me that I win? That I get all I can get? What do my bosses want? Can I accomplish the organization's goal while at the same time establishing a mutually supporting and beneficial relationship? Maybe my sole purpose is to help you, but I cannot do that without interacting with you. The stronger our relationship, the more we can get accomplished. The purpose may very well be just to build a solid relationship, to add a new friend. Because ultimately I need to have relationships to meet my belongingness and esteem needs. I can never have too many.

When building relationships we must understand that relationships do not take place in a vacuum, where two people meet, greet and the relationship is formed, but the environment and its elements dictate how those relationships are formed, how long they will last and often if they are allowed at all. Taking all of the considerations of environment into consideration as well as the elements of self knowledge and empathy, how do we build healthy, mutually beneficial and sustained relationships?

Emotional Intelligence - The Tools of Relationship Building

The tools of relationship building are the competencies and abilities of emotional intelligence. EI, as the tool chest of relationship building, provides the implements and structure for understanding and building mutually beneficial, supportive, and healthy relationships.

The EI tool chest has been built and described in numerous fashions by as many authors and experts. Three of them are mentioned in the beginning of this chapter. Each model or tool chest has its own theory of what the tool chest should contain. Within this chapter we also discuss Nelson and Low and their transformative model of emotional Intelligence. Key to each of the models as well as the model introduced in this article are four basic ideas: first, Every person has a need to recognize one's own self awareness; second; the need to be able to regulate one's own emotions; third; The need to recognize and appreciate the emotions in others; and finally, the ability to exercise the appropriate social skills in each situation. Each of these models is effective at building strong relationships as well as identifying the missing elements in problem relationships. The key to applying these tools is understanding them. What follows is a summary of each of these tool chests which will help you understand the models and choose the best for your situation.

The Tool Chests

The Goleman Model

Highlighted in Figure 9 are Goleman's 4 EI domains and their associated competencies. These domains; Self-Awareness, Self-Management, Social-Awareness, and Relationship Management and their associated competencies, according to Goleman, provide leaders with a sharper understanding of how leadership works and assists them in leading more effectively.[55] Figure 9 provides a listing of each of the EI domains and their associated competencies as identified by Goleman and company in his 2002 book, *Primal Leadership.* Written with co-authors, Richard Boyatzis and Annie McKee, Goleman incorporates the domain of empathy as identified in his benchmark 1995 book, *Emotional Intelligence,* into the domain of Social Awareness thus leaving four overarching domains.

Emotional Intelligence Domains and Competencies
Goleman Model

Personal Competence		Social Competence	
Self Awareness	**Self-Management**	**Social Awareness**	**Relationship Management**
– Emotional Self-Awareness – Self Assessment – Self Confidence	– Emotional Self-Control – Transparency – Adaptability – Achievement – Initiative – Optimism	– Organizational Awareness – Service – Empathy	– Inspirational Leadership – Influence – Developing Others – Catalyst for Change – Conflict Management – Teamwork-collaboration

Fig. 9. Goleman Model of Emotional Intelligence Domains and Competencies

Goleman's four EI domains and 18 leadership competencies are described in these summary definitions from Wikipedia[56]. The first domain is **Self Awareness,** described in short definition as the ability to read one's emotion and recognize the impact while using "gut feelings" to guide decisions. Self Awareness includes the competencies of *emotional self-awareness, accurate self-assessment, and self-confidence.* The second domain is **Self-**

Management. It involves the controlling of one's emotions and impulses and adapting to changing circumstances. Self management includes the competencies of *emotional self-control, transparency, adaptability, achievement, initiative, and optimism.* The third domain is **Social Awareness.** Social Awareness is the ability to sense, understand, and react to others emotions while comprehending social networks. Social Awareness includes the competencies of *empathy, organizational awareness, and service.* The fourth and final domain is **Relationship Management**. This is the ability to inspire, influence and develop others while managing conflict. Relationship management includes the competencies of *inspirational leadership, influence, developing others, being a catalyst for change, conflict management, and teamwork/collaboration.*

In *Primal Leadership* the authors place the domains into two areas of emotional achievement that they ascribe to individuals as they acquire mastery of each domain - Personal Competence and Social Competence. Mastery of the first and second domains, which the authors place under the umbrella of personal competence, depends heavily upon listening to one's self, becoming aware of one's emotional state, values, standards, and the impact one's self awareness or lack thereof impacts others. Self-examination and gathering feedback about oneself through coaching and 360 degree reviews assist with the development of personal competence. Mastery of the third and fourth domains, which the authors describe as social competence, flows from empathic listening and resonating to others' thinking to develop one's thoughts and actions, which enables a leader to provide both unified and individual senses of direction for his or her group. Empathic listening is a skill that requires a basic level of understanding along with regular practice.[57]

The BarOn Model

The BarOn Model is composed of five composite realms and their 15 associated scales. The Interpersonal realm identified by BarOn inherently captures the social competencies of Goleman while BarOn's Intrapersonal, Adaptability, Stress Management and the General Mood realms all focus on the personal competencies. However, the last three provide focus on personal areas not explicitly identified in the Goleman tool chest. The four domains of the Goleman model focus on the two major areas of Personal and Social management; with its 18 competencies all pointing to one or the other of these two major areas, while in the BarOn model the interpersonal realm provides the importance and understanding of relationships and responses to others with the other four realms emphasizing the importance of knowing and managing one's own emotions as the key to orderly and effective relationships.

BarOn Model of Emotional Intelligence

INTRA-PERSONAL	INTER-PERSONAL	ADAPT-ABILITY	STRESS MGMT	GENERAL MOOD
– Emotional Self-Awareness – Assertiveness – Independence – Self-Regard – Self-Actualization	– Empathy – Social Responsibility – Interpersonal Relationship	– Problem Solving – Reality-Testing – Flexibility	– Stress Tolerance – Impulse Control	– Happiness – Optimism

Figure 10. The BarOn Model of Emotional Intelligence.

The 5 Realms of the BarOn construct and their descriptions as found in Stein and Books' *The EQ Edge*[58] are: the **Intrapersonal Realm**, which involves what we generally refer to as the "inner self." It determines how in touch with your feelings you are, how good you feel about yourself and about what you're doing in life. Success in this area means that you are able to express your feelings, live and work independently, feel strong, and have confidence in expressing your ideas and beliefs. The scales under this realm include; *Self-awareness, Assertiveness, Independence, Self-Regard and Self Actualization.* The **Interpersonal Realm** involves what are known as people skills – your ability to interact and get along with others. It includes the scales *of Empathy, Social responsibility and Interpersonal Relationships*. The next realm, the **Adaptability Realm,** involves your ability to be flexible and realistic, and to solve a range of problems as they arise. Its three scales are *Reality Testing, Flexibility and Problem Solving*. The **Stress Management Realm** concerns your ability to tolerate stress and control impulses. Its two scales are *Stress Tolerance and Impulse Control*. The final BarOn realm is the **General Mood Realm**. This realm concerns your general outlook on life. Its two scales are, *Optimism and Happiness.*

The last two models we look at are slightly different in that the Salovey, Mayer, Caruso construct is strictly an abilities model and may be the most pure in providing specific guidance for application of its emotional skills to supporting relationships. The other model is Nelson and Low's Transformative Emotional Intelligence model which although it too is useful to building and sustaining healthy relationships focuses on personal change and success; as the authors explain it in the introduction to their EI textbook.[59] Presented here is the Salovey and Mayer model as it is presented in The Emotionally Intelligent Manager by Peter Salovey and David Caruso.

The emotional intelligence model identified as The Four Skills of Emotional Intelligence in the Salovey and Caruso book is based on the construct of Peter Salovey and John Mayer developed in the 1980's. Presented below in a sequential chart (figure 11), the model as depicted in the authors' book is circular, continuous and hierarchical.

The Four Skills of Emotional Intelligence	
1. Identify Emotion	• Become aware of emotions. • Express emotions.
2. Use Emotions	• Let emotions influence thinking. • Match emotion to the task.
3. Understand Emotion	• Find out what emotion means. • Conduct what –if analyses.
4. Manage Emotion	• Stay open to emotions. • Integrate emotions into thinking.

Fig. 11. The Four Skills of Emotional Intelligence

Below follows a description of the model as it is described in *The Emotionally Intelligent Manager*.[60]

The authors' "intelligent" approach to emotions includes

four different skills arranged in a hierarchical fashion. In their book, the author's state the importance of each of the emotional skills and provide concrete techniques to improve and use the skills in the workplace. The four emotional skills are:

1. Identifying Emotions: *Read people*. Emotions contain data. They are signals to us about important events going on in our world, whether it's your eternal world, social world, or the natural environment. We must accurately identify emotions in others and be able to convey and express emotions accurately to others in order to communicate effectively.

2. Using Emotions: *Get in the Mood.* How we feel influences how we think and what we think about. Emotions direct our attention to important events; they ready us for a certain action and they help guide our thought processes as we solve problems.

3. Understanding Emotions: *Predict the emotional future*. Emotions are not random events. They have underlying causes, they change according to a set of rules, and they

can be understood. Knowledge of emotions is reflected by our emotion vocabulary and our ability to conduct emotional what-if analyses.

4. Managing Emotions: Because emotions contain information and influence thinking, we need to incorporate information and influence thinking we need to incorporate emotions intelligently into our reasoning, problem solving, judging and behaving. This requires us to stay open to emotions whether they are welcome or not, and to choose strategies that include the wisdom of our feelings.

Our final tool chest, The Nelson and Low Transformative Theory of Emotional Intelligence, focuses on emotional intelligence for personal change. Nelson and Low define emotional intelligence as a learned ability to think constructively and behave wisely.[61] Their Emotional Intelligence construct is designed to facilitate that personal change. It is complimented by their Emotional Skills Assessment Process (ESAP) and Experiential Learning System (ELS). The two combined provide a system which first, assesses emotional skills and then provides an intentional process for improving and developing emotional skills. The Nelson and Low construct is composed of Four Competency areas and their 10 related skills. The model also includes three potential problem areas. The chart below depicts the model.

Nelson and Low Model

Competencies and Skills			
Interpersonal Skills	**Leadership Skills**	**Self-Management Skills**	**Intrapersonal Skills**
– Assertion	– Comfort – Empathy – Decision Making – Leadership	– Drive Strength – Time Management – Commitment Ethic	– Self Esteem – Stress Management
Potential Problem Areas			
- Aggression - Deference - Change Orientation			

Fig. 12. Nelson and Low's Transformative model of Emotional Intelligence

The descriptions of the competency areas and skills that follow are as the author's describe them in their 2007 Certification workbook.[62] The authors approach the interpersonal skills competency from a communications perspective with its lone skill being *Assertion*. Describing the **interpersonal competency** they write, "This primary performance area of life consists of the communication skills necessary to establishing and maintaining a variety of strong and healthy relationships. Effective communication is key to positive and healthy relationships." They identify the skill of *assertion* as a powerful, emotional skill that helps communicate more effectively, honestly and appropriately. There are two potential problem areas associated with the assertion skill. These are Aggression and deference. In the case of Aggression there is too much assertion, to the detriment of others and in the case of deference there is not enough assertion which is detrimental to self-esteem. Their second competency, **Leadership skills** is identified in the workbook as Personal Leadership. This area of life consists of the personal and emotional skills essential for developing leadership centered around the person. Personal Leadership is a set of interactive skills, processes, and actions.

Effective leaders create a climate for positively motivating others by knowing, understanding and respecting the needs, values, interests, and goals of others. The skills that enable personal leadership are; *comfort, empathy, decision-making and leadership*. The third competency is Self-Management. They hold that to be successful, satisfied and happy you must learn to motivate yourself and achieve meaningful goals in life, the self management skill of Drive Strength, you must view time as a valuable resource and use time effectively, the skill of time Management, and make commitments and complete projects in a dependable manner which is the skill of commitment ethic. In addition you need to convert a potential problem area of life, change orientation, to the emotional skill of positive personal change. Nelson and Low's final competency area is **Intrapersonal Skills**. The intrapersonal skills are critical to discovering and using your personal belief system toward the betterment of self. The skills in this competency are Self-esteem and Stress Management. These skills include your own private view of confidence, your competence and your abilities.

Conclusions

What emotional intelligence does is take those intangible qualities that facilitate human interaction and interdependence and provide a structure for understanding and applying them to build and support positive, healthy relationships. The variety of Emotional intelligence theories and constructs provide the tools which support the development of those relationships. Simply put, the work that militaries do is hugely dependent on human interaction and influence. Interaction and influence are dependent upon developing and maintaining relationships. Emotional intelligence facilitates developing those relationships.

5. EMOTIONAL INTELLIGENCE, POWER AND INFLUENCE

What is Power and influence?

We begin our discussion of power and influence by turning to the two most famous names surrounding the discussion of power. John French and Bertram Raven state that "The phenomena of power and influence involve a dyadic relation between two agents which may be viewed from two points of view: (a) what determines the behavior of the agent who exerts power? (b) What determines the reactions of the recipient of this behavior?"[63] French and Raven identify the fundamental work of leadership as influencing the actions and reactions of followers. In their language; the leader, the agent who exerts power, and the follower, the agent who is influenced by that application of power. The secret is how the leader determines the method of exercising power. The authors have posed two questions in determining the phenomena of power. The answer to both questions is emotional intelligence. This chapter takes a look at what sources of power are; how sources of power determine levels of commitment and influence and how emotional intelligence guides that influence.

Chapter two began by discounting the myth that all military leaders use a coercive method of influencing followers to accomplish tasks. We also discovered that emotional intelligence empowers leaders to accomplish tasks and develop relationships through other methods. However, coercive methods are one technique available to leaders. We will discuss that among the sources of power, coercion does have a necessary place. We will get to the influence techniques of which coercion is but one. First however let us discuss power and how it is applied by military leaders.

Power. The term itself elicits images of the stern taskmaster lording it over his minions while exerting total domination and control. Fortunately, that is a long way from the actual definition of power. French and Raven describe what has become known as "the most common description of power."[64] Their description focuses on the element of "Social influence" with Social power identified as the capacity to exercise that influence.[65] For the definition of social influence we can refer back to our discussion of the 'phenomena of power as the authors identify social influence as change in belief, attitude, or behavior of a person (the target of influence), which results from the action of another person (an influencing agent).[66] This ties to leadership as the ultimate task of leadership is influencing the actions of others; individuals or groups. So, in a military context power is influence. How do military leaders exert their power to influence others?

Power Bases

Raven and French identify 7 types of power. Mike Clayton, author of the self-help book *Brilliant Influence,* in an online essay discussed these types. Clayton writes, "French and Raven identified seven categories of power, referring to them as Power Bases. They are often divided into two groups: positional power, flowing from the status granted to us; and personal power, which we earn by our endeavors."[67] These power bases are identified in the figure 13 below.

POSITIONAL POWER	PERSONAL POWER
Legitimate Power – Hierarchical authority	Referent Power – Transformational leader
Reward Power – Awards and punishments	Expert Power – Expert knowledge and skills
Coercive Power – Compliance by force	Information power – "It's what you know..."
	Connection Power – "It's who you know..."

Figure 13. French and Raven's Sources of Power

Let us take a deeper look at each of these power bases in turn and how we see them applied in the military environment.

Legitimate power is just that; the reasonable power granted by right of position or legal authority. The commander has legitimate power because he is the commander, the executive officer is the executive officer therefore he has legitimate position power, The First Sergeant is the 1SG and the Squad leader the squad leader; their roles give them legitimate power. Changingminds.org when writing of this French and Raven power base describes legitimate power as that which is invested in a role. Kings, policemen and managers all have legitimate power. The legitimacy may come from a higher power, often one with coercive power. Legitimate power can often thus be the acceptable face of raw power."[68] People are influenced by and respond to the leader purely on the basis of the authority and influence gained from their legitimate power. Leaders operating only from a base of power that is legitimate power succeed in influencing their followers to behave in the manner they are directed and there is no allegiance, as people feel obligated to obedience to the position and there are no long lasting effects or relationship beyond the present or next task. Legitimate power enables the next positional power base, that of Reward power.

Reward power is derived from the follower's belief that a leader has power to provide incentives and rewards that will benefit the follower positively, these rewards range from a paycheck to time off, to a higher position in the organization. Followers are influenced by the perception that if I do well I will be rewarded with good things and my needs will be met as well as the converse; if I do not do well I could lose position, money or prestige. In the military, Reward power is a position power as leaders have and control the ability to provide rewards and incentives as well as punishments. Responding to reward power, followers are influenced only as they see themselves benefiting from the rewards that the leader can provide. With reward power, much like legitimate power, followers are not influenced to achieve any more than they can see themselves rewarded. The withholding of rewards is also a way of influencing followers. This negative use of rewards ties directly to our last positional power base, that of Coercive power.

Coercive power has the potential to be a very abusive power base. Changingminds.org says of coercive power. "This is the power to force someone to do something against their will. It is often physical although other threats may be used. It is the power of dictators, despots and bullies. Coercion can result in physical harm, although its principal goal is compliance. Demonstrations of harm are often used to illustrate what will happen if compliance is not gained."[69] This is the realm of toxic leadership. Toxic leaders often operate from threats and instilling fear into followers. There is never a justification for abuse of position power by using this power base. However, there may be occasions when followers must be forced to comply. There may be situations that are time sensitive or followers may refuse to continue with a mission or task due to fatigue or other stress related factors. The goal is to never use coercive power in an abusive way, however when it is necessary good leaders use it wisely. So, if I should not lean on one or more of the bases of my position power to exert influence, how do I get things done? The answer is personal power.

Personal power, the antithesis of position power, is the influence born of the trust of relationships. Where position power is dictated by my role in the organization, personal power is given by a leader's followers, peers or even superiors. Paul Hershey and Ken Blanchard, two internationally recognized management and leadership experts, define personal power as the extent to which leader's gain the confidence and trust of those people that they're attempting to influence. It's the cohesiveness, commitment, and rapport between leaders and followers.[70] Much like "Transformational Leadership, personal power gets its ability to influence by the degree to which followers see the leader not only being concerned about their individual goals but also as a key link to accomplishing their own goals. French and Raven identified four power bases which make up personal power. These power bases, as identified in figure 13, are described in turn below.

Referent power is the base of power leaders have simply because followers 'like' them. Followers arrive at the conclusion that this is a 'good' leader and is worth following. Hershey and Blanchard refer to this power as the perceived attractiveness of interacting with another person.[71] The key to understanding referent power is by understanding the sources of this "perceived attractiveness." Bruce Avolio in his book, Leadership Development in the Balance provides these sources in his discussion of the leadership styles that describe transformational leadership. He writes, "These style orientations represent a cluster of interrelated styles that characterize leaders who change situations for the better, develop followers into leaders, overhaul organizations to provide them with new strategic directions, and who inspire people by providing an energizing vision and high ideal for moral and ethical conduct."[72] These transformational leaders provide a high level of focus on the needs and development of the individuals that make up the organization and provide connection of individual goals with those of achieving the organizations purpose and development. They let their followers know that they are valued through the characteristics and styles of idealized influence, inspiring leadership, intellectual stimulation and individualized consideration. These are the characteristics they exhibit and are attributed to them and admired by their followers. Figure 14 provides short descriptions of each of these summarized from Avolio's book.

Referent Power and the 4 I's of Transformational Leadership

1. *Idealized Leadership* – These are the people who see the good in others first, and when it is not obvious they work to bring it our through development.

2. *Inspiring Leadership* – They are positively driven leaders who create a positive expectation for success in followers.

3. *Intellectual Stimulation* – The goal of intellectual stimulation is to continuously generate the highest levels of creativity from one's followers.

4. *Individualized Consideration* – This leader spends a lot of time concentrating on the best way to develop his or her people to their full potential, providing the necessary support o accomplish this objective

---

Figure 14. Transformational Leadership and the 4i's

So where do we see referent power in the United States Army? This is the leader represented by The Army's Leadership

Requirement's model. When the Army talks leadership, this is it's ideal leader. This leader is technically and tactically proficient, exemplifies the seven Army values, possesses to a high degree all of the attributes and competencies of the LRM, and is charismatic to the right degree, challenges his or her followers to be critical and creative thinkers and understands how to manage the challenge that is "mission first, people always". Despite its desirability, referent power is not the end all of personal power. Another power base of personal power is expert power.

Expert power is just what it sounds like. It is the recognition by others that this "person" has a degree of expertise in a specific area or areas that makes him or her sought after and held in a higher regard because of those skills. According to Changingminds.org, French and Raven's expert is when individuals have knowledge and skill that someone else requires.[73] This is a very common form of power in the military because of the nature of the profession. There are experts in every occupational specialty and even within these specialties time and experience creates "uber" experts that are often sought after for their superior skills and knowledge. A separate yet related power is information power.

French and Raven's information power is simply the power an individual or groups have due to their access to information. Either they have the information or they have the unique capability to acquire it. They have the access to it. This powerbase is often found with experts along with their expert power. However, it is also found with individuals who have no other powerbase, yet they are sought after and appreciated simply because of the need for the information they hold the access to. Whereas Information power relies on "what they know;" our final powerbase, within personal power, is dependent literally upon who we know.

Connection power, a relative newcomer to the personal power framework, as described by Michael Clayton, comes through networking – being able to use your links to other influential people to support your own, more direct, power. Of course, we may not have much of our own power to supplement – in which case, this becomes little more than reflected glory.[74] We all know people who reflect the power and authority of the people they work for or who they are married to. The battalion commander's favorite company Commander holds a bit of power over his peers because he has the boss's ear. The Family Readiness Group president has pull with the company commanders because she is the brigade commander's spouse. The administrative assistant to the division commander has connection power because of who she works for. This is not because of her position but because of who she knows.

Emotional Intelligence, Power and Influence

So, you ask, what is the role of emotional intelligence within these sources of power? Once again our original question posed by French and Raven at the top of this chapter provides the answer. The question was twofold: (a) what determines the behavior of the agent who exerts power? (b) What determines the reactions of the recipient of this behavior? My response to those questions was emotional intelligence. But how does this work?

Emotional intelligence acts as the enabler for leaders to understand the emotions, attitudes and positions of the personnel they are working with. Leaders who want to establish lasting and positive relationships with others and draw the best out of them use the bases of power that are consequent to personal power, particularly referent power. The use of personal power and referent power is a strong influencer in gaining commitment to a given task, mission or organizational goals, long term and/or short term. Within organizations leaders use referent power to develop resonance within their organization and teams. Goleman, Boyatzis and McKee define resonance as the ability to drive positive feelings in individuals which brings out the best in them. Resonance may very well be described as the opposite to toxicity in organizations. Goleman and company call this toxicity, dissonance, because it is that toxic leader driving the organization by negative feelings.

The two key areas within emotional intelligence which allow the leader to "read' and understand the emotions of others and then in turn act and/or react appropriately are the domains of social awareness and the social skills. Social awareness employs empathy to gain understanding and appreciation of current emotions, attitudes and motivations of others. Then based on this knowledge the appropriate social skills are employed to exert influence to motivate those others to action. Social Skills? What are the social skills in the military and where do we find them. If we revisited the LRM from chapter two, we might identify the skills as the attributes and competencies that enable leaders of character to exercise influence beyond the chain of command and lead others. The Army has gone further fortunately, to identify these social skills. In chapter six of ADRP 6-22, the Army's leadership manual identifies nine social skills which leaders employ to exert influence over others. First, how does the Army define influence and how does it stack up against French and Raven's sources of power? French and Raven discuss the different powerbases within positional and personal power as methods to exert influence over followers. Inherent within each of these power bases are influence tactics. The Army's leadership manual discusses leader's application of influence instead of power. But influence is the application of power. The Army believes influence refers to how people create and relay to others messages, behaviors, and attitudes to affect the intentions, beliefs, behaviors, and attitudes of another person or group of people. Influence depends upon relationships where leaders build positive rapport and a relationship of mutual trust, making followers more willing to support requests. Examples include showing personal interest in a follower's well-being, offering praise, and understanding a follower's perspective. Army leaders have choices in methods of influence based on audience, intent, and expected reaction. The nine skills from ADRP 6-22 are referred to in the manual as methods of influence; they are listed and described in the following table developed from the listing in the ADRP[75].

Methods of Influence
Pressure is applied when leaders use explicit demands to achieve compliance, such as establishing task completion deadlines with negative consequences imposed for unmet completion. This method should be used infrequently since it tends to trigger resentment from followers, especially if the pressure becomes severe. When followers perceive that pressures are not mission-related but originate from their leader's attempt to please superiors for personal recognition, resentment can quickly undermine an organization's morale, cohesion, and quality of performance. Pressure is a good choice when the stakes are high, time is short, and previous attempts at achieving commitment have not been successful.
Exchange is an influence method that leaders use when they make an offer to provide some desired item or action in trade for compliance with a request. Exchange requires that the leaders control certain resources or rewards valued by those being influenced. A four-day pass as reward for excelling during a maintenance inspection is an example of exchange.

Personal appeals occur when the leader asks the follower to comply with a request based on friendship or loyalty. This may be useful in a difficult situation when mutual trust is the key to success. The leader appeals to the follower by highlighting special talents and professional trust for encouragement before taking on a tough mission. An S3 might ask a staff officer to brief at an important commander's conference if the S3 knows the staff officer will do the best job conveying information.

Collaboration occurs when the leader cooperates in providing assistance or resources to carry out a directive or request. The leader makes the choice more attractive by being prepared to step in and resolve problems. A major planning effort before a deployment for humanitarian assistance would require possible collaboration with unified action partners.

Rational persuasion requires the leader to provide evidence, logical arguments, or explanations showing how a request is relevant to the goal. This is often the first approach to gaining compliance or commitment from followers and is likely to be effective if the leader is recognized as an expert in the specialty area in which the influence occurs. Leaders often draw from their own experience to give reasons why some tasks can be accomplished because the leader has tried it and done it.

Apprising happens when the leader explains why a request will benefit a follower, such as giving greater satisfaction in their work or performing a task a certain way that will save time. In contrast to exchange, the benefits are out of the control of the leader. A commander may use the apprising method to inform a newly assigned NCO that serving in a staff position, before serving as a platoon sergeant, could provide invaluable experience. The commander points out that the additional knowledge may help the NCO achieve higher performance and possibly lead to an accelerated promotion.

Legitimating occurs when leaders establish their authority as the basis for a request when it may not be obvious. In the military, certain jobs must be done regardless of circumstances when subordinate leaders receive legitimate orders from higher headquarters. Reference to one's position suggests to those being influenced that there is the potential for official action if the request is not completed.

Inspirational appeals occur when the leader fires up enthusiasm for a request by arousing strong emotions to build conviction. A leader may stress to a fellow leader that without help, the safety of the team may be at risk. By appropriately stressing the results of stronger commitment, a unit leader can inspire followers to surpass minimal standard s and reach elite performance status.

Participation occurs when the leader asks others to take part in his processes to address a problem or meet an objective. Active participation leads to an increased sense of worth and recognition. It provides value to the effort and builds commitment to execute. By involving key leaders at all levels during planning, senior leaders ensure that their followers take stock in the vision. These subordinates will later be able to pursue critical intermediate and long-term

Figure 15. Methods of influence. ADRP 6-22

Conclusions

In this chapter we looked at the sources and bases of power, discussed their implications for the U.S. Army and discussed the role of emotional intelligence in identifying appropriate sources of power and the selection of the appropriate methods of influence for a specific situation.

French and Raven identified the fundamental work of leadership as influencing the actions and reactions of followers. Effective leaders know how to influence their followers to ensure success; not just for the completion of tasks, but also workers who understand and are committed to the task and mission. The key to both of these elements of success is leaders who possess the emotional intelligence to choose the right influence methods.

6. Emotional Intelligence and Resilience in the United States Army

*"**Resilience:** showing a tendency to recover quickly from setbacks, shock, injuries, adversity, and stress while maintaining a mission and organizational focus." ADRP 6-22 – Army Leadership, Confident, Competent, and Agile*

"You're going to see in the next probably 90 -120 days that we'll come out with a comprehensive fitness program, Comprehensive Soldier Fitness. What we realize is that we need to bring mental fitness to the same level of attention that we give to physical fitness because we're dealing with the realities of war. You can build resilience in mental fitness just like you can build resilience with pushups."

Chief of Staff of the Army General George W. Casey Jr. at AUSA ILW Breakfast, 14 January 2009.

"After eight years of war, we must better prepare our Soldiers and their Families to persevere with the challenges inherent to military service. The key to increased resiliency is placing the same level of enthusiasm toward conditioning our minds and souls as we place toward conditioning our bodies."
Brig. Gen. Ed Cardon, Deputy Commandant, Command and General Staff College - CGSC CSF Webpage

In October 2006, the Army's revised Leadership doctrine became official with the publication of Field Manual 6-22 (this regulation has since been recast as Army Doctrine Reference Publication (ADRP) 6-22 in 2012, with the most significant change being the addition of two new competencies and the moniker of ADRP). The new leadership framework introduced by FM6-22 highlighted twelve leader attributes and eight leader competencies; what the leader needs to Be/know and Do. Listed within the Leadership attributes is the leader behavior resilience. ADRP 6-22 says of resilient leaders, "Resilient leaders can recover quickly from setbacks, shock, injuries, adversity, and stress while maintaining their mission and organizational focus. Their resilience rests on will, the inner drive that compels them to keep going, even when exhausted, hungry, afraid, cold, and wet. Resilience helps leaders and their organizations to carry difficult missions to their conclusion." [76] This was the first recognition of the importance of resilience in Army Leadership doctrine. Unfortunately the four short paragraphs in field manual 6-22 and now the ADRP only look at one aspect of resilience; that of leaders in combat. Fortunately, the Army recognized the need for resiliency beyond the battlefield and not just for Soldiers but for all members of the Army family. The necessity for strengthening this vital behavior has become more significant because of the stress on the force of more than 13 years of war. The Casey and Cardon quotes illustrate the increased importance Army leadership has placed on Soldier resiliency and the major steps taken towards helping not just the leadership but all of the Army family to attain greater levels of resiliency.   The key element of the increased recognition and intent to build resiliency in the force was the introduction in 2008 of the Comprehensive Soldier Fitness initiative.

The Army's Comprehensive Soldier Fitness (CSF) initiative has as its' goal to build resiliency not just in leaders but in all of the members of the Army family. In March, 2014 the Army changed the name of its resiliency initiative to Comprehensive soldier and Family Fitness (CSF2) to add emphasis to the fact that this was a holistic program. CSF, According to the CGSC CSF Website, enables Soldiers, Families, and Army Civilians to have increased resilience through a holistic approach that ensures a healthy, balanced force that excels in an era of high operational tempo and persistent conflict.[77] The CSF program's stated purpose, as outlined in the 2009 Army Posture Statement is to; enhance resilience, [which is] achieved by a combination of specific training and improved fitness in the five domains of health, can decrease post-traumatic stress, decrease the incidence of undesirable and destructive behaviors, and lead to a greater likelihood for post-adversity growth and success.[78] The program has identified five dimensions of health: Emotional, Social, Spiritual, Family, and Physical fitness (defined in figure 1) as the key areas to maintain in instilling and increasing resiliency. The goal is to build strength and fitness in each dimension: thereby increasing individual, family, unit and Army resiliency.

5 DIMENSIONS OF STRENGTH

Physical- Performing and excelling in physical activities that require aerobic fitness, endurance, strength, healthy body composition, and flexibility derived through exercise, nutrition and training

Emotional - Approaching life's challenges in a positive, optimistic way by demonstrating self-control, stamina, and good character with your choices and actions.

Social - Developing and maintaining trusted, valued relationships and friendships that are personally fulfilling and foster good communication including a comfortable exchange of ideas, views, and experiences.

Family - Being part of a family unit that is safe, supportive and loving, and provides the resources needed for all members to live in a healthy and secure environment.

> **Spiritual** - Strengthening a set of beliefs, principles or values that sustain a person beyond family, institutional, and societal sources of strength.

Figure 16. The Five Dimensions of Strength[79]

The Army developed, along with the University of Pennsylvania, a comprehensive plan to conduct training to build resiliency, through building strength in each dimension. Each of these dimensions are impacted by how balanced an individual is in his understanding and confidence in himself, her relationships with others and his or her environment. To address each of these elements holistically the Army's comprehensive fitness programs must include awareness and training in Emotional Intelligence (EI).

How Emotional Intelligence can make a difference.

According to Dr. Reuven Baron, emotional intelligence addresses the emotional, personal, social and survival dimensions of intelligence, which are often more important for daily functioning than the more traditional cognitive aspects of intelligence. Emotional intelligence is concerned with understanding oneself and others, relating to people, and adapting to and coping with the immediate surroundings to be more successful in dealing with environmental demands.[80]

Although only one of the strength dimensions deals specifically with Soldier and Family emotions; emotions, and emotional intelligence are inherent in each of the dimensions and finds its way into every area of an individual's life. This holistic nature of emotional intelligence is the very reason it can influence resiliency in a positive manner. Reivich and Shatte' in recognition of the importance of EI to resiliency wrote in *The Resilience Factor*, "While not much can be done to improve your IQ, a lot can be done to improve your resilience, a key component of emotional intelligence." [81] Understanding the competencies of emotional intelligence and making personal application of EI to an individual's life will increase comprehensive fitness and resiliency.

Emotional intelligence is about understanding your own emotions and those of others in order to be a more successful person. The emotionally well-balanced person will be successful in the sense that she will anticipate adversity and its impacts; personally, professionally, relationally and the potential responses of others. This anticipation will allow them to develop the appropriate responses and bounce back quickly. Dr. Reuven BarOn, an expert in the field, identified the importance of EI to individual success and coping in his 1997 publication, *The EQ-i Technical Manual*. In his manual he writes, *"Emotional intelligence is concerned with understanding oneself and others, relating to people, and adapting to and coping with the immediate surroundings to be more successful in dealing with environmental demands."*[82] Here the author speaks directly to the ability of EI to assist individuals in dealing with the stressors of their environment by understanding their emotions as well as the emotions of others. Although there are a number of EI experts and models that could also provide valid assistance to resiliency training, BarOn's model clearly, best addresses the areas of concern for Soldier resiliency. The model in figure 17 below and the discussion addresses the application of the model to building and maintaining resiliency. The realm descriptions in the model are as highlighted in *The EQ Edge*, by Steven J. Stein and Howard E. Book.

BarOn Model of Emotional Intelligence

INTRA-PERSONAL	INTER-PERSONAL	ADAPT-ABILITY	STRESS MGMT	GENERAL MOOD
– Emotional Self-awareness – Assertiveness – Independence – Self-Regard – Self – Actualization	– Empathy – Social Responsibility – Interpersonal Relationship	– Problem Solving – Reality-Testing – Flexibility	– Stress Tolerance – Impulse Control	– Happiness – Optimism
EFFECTIVE PERFORMANCE				

Figure 17. The BarOn Model of Emotional Intelligence.

The BarOn Model defines the emotional intelligence competencies in five key composite realms with 15 subscales. These realms and subscales highlight the major areas of focus for improving Soldier resiliency.

Although they have major application to each of the CSF domains as they relate to resiliency, two of BarOn's EI realms more directly affect the CSF dimensions of emotional and social fitness. These two areas are BarOn's Interpersonal realm and The Intrapersonal realm.

The CSF social dimension is primarily addressed by BarOn's **Interpersonal realm.** This realm captures the three key areas in which Soldiers need to attain competency in order to have and maintain orderly and effective relationships. These relationships define how effective a Soldier will be in the social dimension. By recognizing, the issues that surround him or her in regards to interacting with others and acting to develop any shortcomings will improve a Soldier's resiliency. This realm's three subscales, empathy, social responsibility and interpersonal relationship address the social competencies that when exercised effectively leads to successful interaction with others. The others this refers to is not just work and job relationships; but includes family, neighbors, teachers, coaches, mentors ; anyone who is part of the Soldier's life. Whereby the interpersonal realm affects relationships with others, BarOn's intrapersonal realm assists the Soldier in becoming more aware of his own emotions.

The **Intrapersonal Realm**, which involves what we generally refer to as the "inner self," determines how in touch with your feelings you are, how good you feel about yourself and about what you're doing in life. Success in this area means that you are able to express your feelings, live and work independently, feel strong, and have confidence in expressing your ideas and beliefs. The scales under this realm include; Self-awareness, Assertiveness, Independence, Self-Regard and Self Actualization. This realm allows the Soldier to develop true self-awareness of his or her strengths, weaknesses, fears and builds the ability to deal with each of these through self-awareness.

Each of the remaining three realms of BarOn's model add emphasis to the importance of developing personal emotionally intelligent fitness as they each deal with areas in which the individual has to develop personal competency and strength which leads to personal resiliency. These realms are *Adaptability, Stress Management, and General Mood*.

The first of these, the **Adaptability Realm,** involves the ability to be flexible and realistic, and to solve a range of problems as they arise. It addresses the Soldiers ability to size up and respond to a wide range of difficult situations. [83] Its three scales are Reality Testing, Flexibility, and Problem Solving. It is readily apparent how addressing this area is necessary to developing resiliency as it deals directly with the ability to identify and deal with problems and unexpected events. The **Stress Management Realm** concerns an individual's ability to tolerate stress and control impulses. This realm addresses the ability to withstand stress without caving in, falling apart, losing control, or going under.[84] Its two scales are Stress Tolerance and Impulse Control. Stress tolerance addresses the ability of the individual to withstand adverse events and stressful situations without developing physical or emotional symptoms by actively and positively coping with stress[85]. Impulse control addresses the ability to resist or delay an impulse, drive, or temptation to act.[86] This ability determines how well an individual makes decisions by first considering alternatives and consequences. The final realm is the **General Mood Realm**. This realm is influenced heavily by how well an individual performs in the other realms. It concerns an individual's outlook on life, her ability to enjoy herself and others and overall feelings of contentment or dissatisfaction.[87] Its two scales describe this realm, the scales of Optimism and Happiness, and extols the advantages to having a positive outlook on life.

Emotional Intelligence Assessment and Training

Assessment is the first step in development. In order to use emotional intelligence to develop and improve resiliency there must obviously be a starting place. Although it is a relatively new field of study, there are a host of very good EI assessment instruments and EI education and development programs. One of these is Dr BarOn's Emotional Quotient Inventory (EQ-i). The EQ-i measures an individual's level of emotional intelligence and provides an assessment report that suggests a development program to build on areas of weakness. The other advantage of the EQ-i, is that it must be administered by and its results presented to the individual by a certified coach/counselor. This counselor also assists the individual in understanding the report and developing a program to improve.

EI and Resiliency: It's a No Brainer

People are inherently emotional and social creatures, gaining their motivations and satisfactions from other people and from the level of success, they attain while interacting with the environment. The current operational environment with its attendant optempo has increased the pressures on the force causing a requirement to place more emphasis on the need to ensure and build resiliency in individuals. The Army CSF2 initiative has been developed for that purpose. However, a vital piece is missing from current CSF training. A logical response to the need for training in emotional social creatures is to address the emotional aspects to develop resiliency. The very nature of emotional intelligence causes an individual to gain strength by proactively acknowledging their emotions and the foundations of their development. Once an individual has recognized that there are emotionally intelligent areas, where they may have a shortfall or need improvement they can further exercise the ability to get stronger.

7. EMOTIONAL INTELLIGENCE FOR MILITARY LEADERS - CONCLUSIONS

This book has attempted to provide an overview of the importance of Emotional Intelligence to military leaders by offering some basic information on how EI can make a difference in military organizations. This has not been meant to be the end all of Emotional intelligence for the military, it is merely a start to raise the awareness of military leaders to this valuable and available tool of leadership. The intent was to show how EI can make a positive impact in several key areas of leadership. To that end we identified several areas and issues where Emotional Intelligence can be a factor.

1. *Emotional Intelligence is a Key competency for Army Leaders.*

Chapters one and two identified the place of emotional intelligence in the Army's Leadership Requirements Model and made the case that the Army has recognized the need for EI to develop well rounded leaders for the future.

2. Emotional Intelligence is key to building healthy and sustained relationships.

Chapter three discussed the role of EI and interdependence in relationship building. In it we identified the importance of Self-knowledge, Empathy and understanding the environment in order to build relationships that are valued and lasting.

3. The fundamental task of Leaders is influencing the actions and reactions of followers.

In chapter four we examined how power and influence work by discussing the sources of power and the role of EI as the agent that determines how to choose the appropriate sources of power and influence techniques.

4. Emotional Intelligence is the tonic to toxic leadership

In chapter five we discussed how emotional intelligence training can help solve the problem of toxic leadership in military organizations, by raising the self awareness of toxic leaders and providing training on EI skills.

5. Self Awareness is the first step to building and strengthening personal Resiliency.

In chapter 6 we traced the development of the U.S. Army's Comprehensive Soldier Fitness program for building resiliency and addressed how Emotional Intelligence can be a key component of the program. We showed how EI can make a difference, beginning first with developing personal self-awareness.

Why Emotional Intelligence for Leaders?

Every leader possesses emotional intelligence and emotional intelligence impacts a wide range of leadership requirements. Leaders that have a high degree of emotional intelligence understand that EI enhances every area of leadership and organizational operations. Emotional Intelligence provides a solid pathway to effective leadership, successful relationships, and winning teams and organizations.

[1] Salovey and Mayer. Emotional Intelligence, (New York: Baywood Publishing Company, Inc. 1990), p. 189, 190.
[2] Goleman, Daniel, Emotional Intelligence 1995.
[3] Goleman, Daniel, "What Makes a Leader", Harvard Business Review – The Best of HBR 1998, (January 2004): p2-10
[4] Goleman, Daniel, *Working With Emotional Intelligence*, (Bantam Books, New York, New York 1998). P317
[5] Goleman, Boyatzis and McKee, *Primal Leadership*,(Harvard Business School Press, Boston, Massachusetts,2002). P6.
[6] Field Manual 6-22, *Army Leadership*. (Headquarters, Department of the Army, October 2006.), p. 1-2.
[7] Goleman, Daniel, "What Makes a Leader", Harvard Business Review, (Nov-Dec 1998): p93-102.
[8] FM 6-22, pg 1-2.
[9] Gardner, Howard. *Frames of Mind*, (New York: Basic Books Inc., 1983), p. 12.
[10] BarOn, Reuven, *BarOn Emotional Quotient Inventory, Technical Manual*, (New York: Multi-Health Systems, 1997), p. 2.
[11] Gardner, 1983, p. 239.
[12] Ibid.
[13] Salovey and Mayer, p. 189, 190.
[14] Salovey and Mayer, p. 185.
[15] Goleman, Daniel, "What Makes a Leader", Harvard Business Review, (Nov-Dec 1998): p93-102.
[16] Ibid.
[17] Goleman, Boyatzis and McKee, *Primal Leadership*, (Boston, Mass: Harvard Business School Press, 2002) p. 38.
[18] Ibid, p.37-38
[19] http://en.wikipedia.org/wiki/Emotional_Intelligence, retrieved 29 December 2008
[20] Businesslistening.com, (http://www.businesslistening.com/primal-leadership-2.php#emotional-intelligence-leadership-competencies, retrieved 5 March 2008)
[21] Stein and Book, *The EQ Edge*, (Canada: Jossey-Bass), p. 22 - 23, 2006.
[22] FM6-22 p. 6-4.
[23] Ibid, p. 8-8.
[24] Goleman, Boyatzis and McKee .30. 2002.
[25] Ibid, pg iii
[26] TRADOC Pam 525-3-7=01, *Human Dimension in the Future 2015-2024*, (Headquarters, Department of the Army, April, 2008) p. 9.
[27] Ibid, p. 16.
[28] Human dimension Defined at AUSA, http://www.army.mil/-

news/2008/10/09/13197-human-dimension-defined-at-ausa/, retrieved 7 March 2009
[29] TRADOC Pam, p. 7.
[30] FM6-22, p. 2-4.
[31] Ibid, p. A-1
[32] Ibid, p. A-10
[33] Broaddus and McCullum, "Leader-imposed Stress in Organizations: Do You Improve Your Organization, or Detract From its Success?" USACGSOC curriculum, Lesson L106, 2014.
[34] Reed George R, "Toxic Leadership", Military Review, July-August 2004, pages 67 to 71.
[35] Army Leader Development Strategy 2013, (Headquarters Department of the Army, 2013) p.3.
[36] Goleman, Boyatzis and McKee, P15.
[37] Zeidner, Matthews, Roberts, *What we know about Emotional Intelligence*, (The MIT Press, Cambridge Massachusetts, 2009) p.283.
[38] Goleman, Boyatzis and McKee, p.x.
[39] Army Doctrine Reference Publication 6-22, *Army Leadership*. (Headquarters, Department of the Army, August 2012.), p. 1-1.
[40] Goleman, Boyatzis and McKee. P39
[41] Zeidner, Matthews, and Roberts, *What We Know about Emotional Intelligence*, (MIT Press, Cambridge, Massachusetts, 2009), 25.
[42] Ibid.
[43] Ibid. 26.
[44] Ibid. 27.
[45] Salovey and Mayer, "Imagination, Cognition and Personality", (Baywood Publishing Co., Inc. Amity, New York, 1990), 189.
[46] http://en.wikipedia.org/wiki/Interdependence
[47] http://psychclassics.yorku.ca/Maslow/motivation.htm
[48] http://answers.ask.com/Science/Biology/what_is_interdep...
[49] http://en.wikipedia.org/wiki/Interdependence
[50] http://psychclassics.yorku.ca/Maslow/motivation.htm
[51] Ibid.
[52] Goleman, Boyatzis and McKee, *Primal Leadership*, (Harvard Business Review Press, Boston Massachusetts, 2002), 30.
[53] Darwin Nelson, Gary Low, *Emotional Intelligence: Achieving Academic and Career Excellence*, (Prentice Hall, Boston Massachusetts, 2nd ed., 2011), 20.
[54] Covey, Stephen R., *The Seven Habits of Highly Effective People*, (Simon and Schuster, New York, New York 1989), 235.http://en.wikipedia.org/wiki/Emotional_Intelligence, retrieved 29 December 2008
[55] http://en.wikipedia.org/wiki/Emotional_Intelligence, retrieved 29 December 2008. Businesslistening.com, (http://www.businesslistening.com/primal-leadership-2.php#emotional-intelligence-leadership-competencies, retrieved 5 March 2008)
[56] Businesslistening.com, (http://www.businesslistening.com/primal-leadership-

2.php#emotional-intelligence-leadership-competencies, retrieved 5 March 2008)
[57] Stein and Book, *The EQ Edge*, (Canada: Jossey-Bass), p. 22 - 23, 2006
[58]. Nelson and Low, xxvii.
[59] Salovey and Caruso, The Emotionally Intelligent Manager, (Jossey-Bass, San Francisco, Ca, 2004), x
[60] Darwin Nelson, Gary Low, Ross Ellis, "Emotional Intelligence: A Transformative Theory and Applied Model for Positive Personal Change," Emotional Intelligence (EI) Theory, Research and Practice, (2010): 10-14.
[61] Ibid pg 84
[62] Darwin Nelson, Gary Low, and Richard Hammett, *Emotional Intelligence and Personal Excellence: Building quality from Within*, (EI Learning Systems, Inc. Kingsville, TX, 2007), 1-7.
[63] Zimmer, French and Raven's Source of Power, http://zimmer.csufresno.edu/~johnca/spch100/9-6-french.htm
[64] *French and Ravens Forms of Power*, http://changingminds.org/explanations/power/french_and_raven.htm
[65] Ibid.
[66] Ibid
[67] Clayton, Mike, Brilliant Influence, http://brilliantinfluence.wordpress.com/2010/08/19/*french-and-ravens-power-bases/*
[68] http://changingminds.org/explanations/power/french_and_raven.htm
[69] Ibid.
[70] Paul Hershey and Kenneth Blanchard, Management of Organizational Behavior: Utilizing Human Resources, (Prentice-Hall, Inc., Englewood Cliffs, NJ, 1988), 206
[71] Ibid., 210
[72] Avolio, Bruce, Leadership Development in Balance: Made/Born, (Lqwrence Erbaum Associates, Publishers, Mahwah, NJ 2005), 195
[73] Changingminds.org.
[74] Clayton, Mike.
[75] Army Defense Reference Publication 6-22, (Headquarters Department of the Army, August 2013.), 6-2.
[76] Field Manual 6-22, *Army Leadership*. (Headquarters, Department of the Army, October 2006.), p. 5-3.
[77] https://courses.leavenworth.army.mil/webapps/portal/frameset.jsp, retrieved October 22, 2009.
[78] http://www.army.mil/aps/09/information_papers/comprehensive_soldier_fitness_program.html, retrieved October 22, 2009.
[79] http://www.army.mil/csf/, retrieved November 24, 2009.
[80] BarOn, Reuven, *BarOn Emotional Quotient Inventory, Technical Manual*, (New York: Multi-Health Systems, 1997), p. 2.
[81] Karen Reivich and Andrew Shatte', The Resilience Factor, (New York: Broadway Books, 2002), p18.
[82] BarOn, p. 2.
[83] Steven J Stein and Howard Book, The EQ Edge-Emotional Intelligence and Your Success,(Ontario: Josey-Bass, 2006)p.161

[84] Ibid, p. 189.
[85] Ibid, p. 191.
[86] Ibid, p. 204.
[87] Ibid, p. 215.

Printed in Great Britain
by Amazon.co.uk, Ltd.,
Marston Gate.